SHOES OF THE SHOAH

THE TOMORROW OF YESTERDAY

DOROTHY PIERCE

ISBN: 9789493056787 (ebook)
ISBN: 9789493056770 (paperback)

Publisher: Amsterdam Publishers

info@amsterdampublishers.com

Holocaust Survivor True Stories WWII , Book 5

CONTENTS

In Loving Memory of

Henny Fletcher Aronson

November 25, 1924 - January 1, 2019

INTRODUCTION

I am not a writer. I used to be a mathematician before age deprived me of that ability. I am, however, a Jew. Not just a Jew, but a Jew obsessed with preserving my heritage, my culture, my Holocaust. So, when I discovered that a friend of mine was a Holocaust survivor who – because she thought there was no interest – refused to share her experience with others, it became apparent that my friend Henny's story had to be told.

I know that many Holocaust books are out there, so why another? It is my firm belief that there can never be enough told about the Holocaust because each story is different. Each adds to the accumulation of our history, each gives us a different lesson, each reveals a hidden fact and each reminds us of what should never be forgotten. Henny's story adds new insight into our history. Her story is about Lithuania, the Kovno ghetto, the Stutthof concentration camp, a death march, survival, and eventual victory over adversity.

The story begins with her death march and the recollections about her life before the German invasion of Kovno. We follow Henny as she matures and we learn about her family and school life. We are with her when she is forced into the ghetto with her family and meets and marries her husband, Raphael (also called Ralph), while in the ghetto. We learn about Raphael and his family. We listen to Henny's voice as she recounts the abuse of the Jews by the Lithuanians, the German atrocities, the sadistic *Aktions*, and we cry with her at her losses.

We are with Henny as she tries to hide from the Germans, is sent to Stutthof concentration camp, where she sees and experiences the horror of starvation, death, and disease surrounding her, faces her own death, loses her parents, uncles, cousins and her brother.

Through her voice, we experience her liberation by the Russians and eventually finding her way to Lodz where she is reunited with Raphael. We follow Henny as she and her husband weave their way through Europe and eventually relocate to the United States. We learn of their life and successes there.

Henny's story is about courage, hope, and the will to live. It is a story that must be shared with the world. It is a lesson for students about how a young person survived the most horrific treatment imaginable and triumphed.

We spent many hours recounting Henny's story on videotape. She amazed me with her ability to recall so many incidents and when I mentioned this, she stated, "It is often more difficult to forget than to remember. We'll never forget the unpleasant experiences. It is almost like a deep wound that never heals, but in time it develops a crust."

Henny's story is recounted in the pages that follow. Much of her story is in her own words.

It has been very difficult for me to write this memoir. Reading and hearing about the atrocities carried out by the Germans brought tears to my eyes and filled me with intense anger and hatred. I don't know how, but it is indeed a miracle that Henny survived.

I am honored to present her story and in doing so, I very much hope that her story of survival will contribute to the important knowledge base of the horrendous Holocaust.

Henny is gone from us now, but her story will live on and continue to inspire those in the direst conditions and to remind us what we as humans are capable of doing.

I would like to thank Henny's son, Steven Aronson, for all his assistance, editing, encouragement, and photographs. I would also like to thank Tina Aronson, Henny's daughter, for her contribution to this memoir.

Dorothy Pierce

I. WINTER 1945

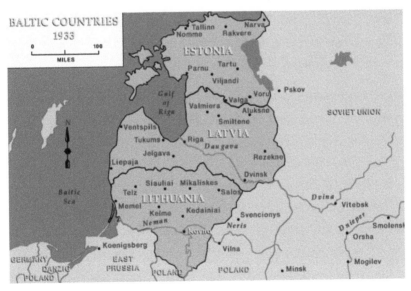

Baltic Countries, 1933, Kovno Indicated. No date. US Holocaust
Memorial Museum.

*If you listened carefully, you could distinguish between the
footprints and the water as the ghostly group snaked along the
river. You could hear the worn and frightened heartbeats. No*

1

fruitless cries for mothers, long stifled by despair, or hunger pains from stomachs deprived of nourishment could be heard. You couldn't see the hair falling from sallow coatless skulls, but if you looked, really looked, you could see the desperation, terror, resignation, and horror on their once youthful, now skeletal faces. They marched, never ceasing, barely breathing, always knowing that the slightest hesitation would bring instant death.

Henny, barely 20 years old, marched with them and you could feel her determination as she willed herself onward. She wouldn't give Hitler the satisfaction of killing her – wherever he was in hell. If you could read minds you would know that she thought only of survival.

They trudged through unfamiliar country sides speckled with barns, fences, farmhouses, forests, and stacks of hay. They stepped over pockets of mud, torn branches, large boulders, icy ponds, dead flowers, and bodies.

As she saw the battered bodies fall, Henny thought of how she was constantly surrounded by death, disease, and corpses. They were something she had become accustomed to – they had become part of her life. She thought of this horrible experience and how unbelievable and unthinkable it was that people could be so terribly cruel. They were so young, the ones marching and killing them, probably younger than she was. How terrible it was to admit; when Henny saw some girls lying on the snow, being shot, it had become an everyday thing.

Henny would have died had it not been for the incident with the shoes, but that is for later. For now, she would think back to the beginning.

II. YESTERDAY

"Fiction cannot recite the numbing numbers, but it can be that witness, that memory. A storyteller can attempt to tell the human tale, can make a galaxy out of the chaos, can point to the fact that some people survived even as most people died. And can remind us that the swallows still sing around the smokestacks."
Jane Yolen

It's been over 70 years and I can still remember 1941 in detail when the year the civilized world went mad. The Germans decided to eradicate Jewish people while the rest of the world stood by and claimed ignorance. According to Hitler, we were not supposed to survive, but we were lucky.

This story must be told so I decided to record my life for my children and grandchildren. I want them to know how fortunate they are to have grandparents because I, like so many others, lost my grandparents amongst the madness. This is not only a story about humanity's cruelty but also about losing faith in people and their kindness.

Perhaps, there were those who were against these atrocities but believed they could not do anything but follow orders and keep quiet. Nevertheless, they continued to show incredible brutality towards innocent people who had no way of protecting themselves.

My arrival into this world was in 1924, during the wonderful 20-year period of Lithuania's independence. During World War I, Lithuania was occupied by German troops but in 1918, Lithuania declared its independence and in 1920, under the Treaty of Moscow, Russia officially recognized this independence.

During Lithuania's 20-year independence, Kovno (Kaunas) became the capital and because of its geographical and strategic position, on the right bank of the Neman River, the city developed into the administrative and economic center of the surrounding area.

Kovno was the central hub of the Ministry for Jewish Affairs, the Jewish National Council, and other Lithuanian Jewish organizations. Five Jewish newspapers were published daily in Kovno, including the Zionist daily *Yidishe Shtime*, founded in 1919. Thirty-five thousand Jews resided and supported three full-time Hebrew and one Yiddish gymnasium, a folk theater, a Hebrew theatrical studio, 40 synagogues, a Jewish hospital, and numerous youth organizations. Kovno was also an important Zionist center.

For the next two decades, Lithuania flourished both economically and culturally. Jews in all professions, especially lawyers, contributed to the independence and subsequent prosperity of the country. The government approved private schools for minorities and for students to be taught in their own language. A commercial

Yiddish high school (*Yiddische Kommerz Gimnazia*) set up clubs for the students, as well as a kindergarten and an elementary school. Hebrew language instruction was either *Tarbut* (secular) while religious education in Hebrew was called *Yavneh*. There was also secular education in Yiddish.

The people involved with boosting Lithuania's economy entered into business deals with German companies and Germany was eager to cooperate in order to help its own economy. Many Lithuanian business people, including my father, represented German companies. It was a prosperous time for the Lithuanian Jews. Then, in 1933, Adolf Hitler became chancellor of Germany and his book *Mein Kampf*, originally published in 1925-26, became available for all to read, not only Germans. The book grew enormously in popularity and, under its influence, Lithuanians began to believe that prosperity was available if you killed the Jews and limited their freedom and practices.

My childhood was wonderful. My father owned a bookstore and we lived behind it. He was a devout Yiddishist and sold non-religious Jewish books by the likes of Sholem Rabinovitsh, Sholem Abramovitsh, and I.L. Peretz. He was always trying to acquire and sell as many Jewish books as possible. His store was more like a library, people spent hours reading and perusing the shelves.

The bookstore closed down, I was told, when I was about a year old when my mother went shopping and left my father to look after me. She left me on their large bed, a place she considered safest for her beautiful little girl. The store bell chimed and when my father, always eager to greet customers, went to answer it, he forgot about me and I fell off the bed. He was so upset with himself that he took the customer by the shoulders, threw him out, and closed the bookstore down. I'm not sure how successful he was anyway, Jews from all over would visit the store and take up residence in the musty bookshelves but would never buy any of the books.

Ever resourceful, my father went into business selling educational toys and games, like chess and checkers. He then represented a German company selling dolls and toys for children. I thought I was the luckiest girl alive because I was given samples of the beautiful dolls my father was selling.

We moved into an apartment on Vilnius Street, in an affluent area of Kovno. A big post office was at the entrance to our building and a wonderful kosher delicatessen, that sold excellent hot dogs, was across the street. By car, you would drive through the entrance into a courtyard surrounded by apartments. Our apartment was on the second floor and had a large interior with an enormous warehouse in the back, where my father ran his business. He would often travel for work and once, while in Vilna, he bought me a magnificent glass dollhouse filled with glass furniture. I treasured that dollhouse and was so protective of it. When I went to school, I would have to lock my bedroom door to prevent my younger brother from sneaking in and playing with it.

The books from the store were moved to the apartment, so we had a library filled with hundreds of well-known Jewish books. The apartment had a small maisonette in the kitchen, just big enough for one person to sleep in. Our maid would climb up a ladder and sleep in this maisonette when her daily chores were completed. One of my favorite stories was when I was about four years old and there was a fire in the apartment. While escaping the blaze, my mother had handed me to my father but instead of leaving, he put me on the dining room table and ran to the kitchen. He had built a little box under the maid's mattress to keep his money safe. You can imagine the argument that ensued between my parents when my father left me to save his money.

Henny's Mother. Date unknown. Courtesy of Steve Aronson.

My mother was lovely. It is difficult for me to talk about her, even after all these years. She was pretty, soft-spoken, polite, and well educated. She came from a small town while my father came from Vilna. He was a swinger, sharp-minded, and was educated but didn't attend university. He was a wonderful man, a true Yiddishist, an entrepreneur who loved enterprise, reading, writing, and bad jokes. He was a happy man and his happiness was infectious. My father even recorded his jokes on the back of each tear-off page of the Jewish calendar.

Most days, when I came home from school, I would find my father with three or four people discussing world issues and the need for new games for children. He brought home smart and hungry men and my mother always served them tea and jam. I remember one man was a deaf-mute and my father would write instructions for him on his hand. My father was completely preoccupied with creating new children's educational games and amassed a plethora of them. He employed good craftsmen who built the most beautiful chess, checkers, and domino games. Because of his enthusiasm and perseverance, my father was successful in business and this earned my family a place among the upper class.

The highlight of my young life came every December when I, along with some friends, would help my father deliver packed orders to customers whose businesses were on the high street. We hired a sled with a driver, drawn by horses. The orders were placed on the sled, with us covered with heavy furs, and we would stop at every store to make the deliveries. I would say that I was Fletcher's daughter and the customer would give me the money. My father had a lot of faith in me and, at the age of ten or eleven, he thought I could do anything. This instilled a tremendous amount of self-confidence in me and helped me during and after the war. My father told me that if I wanted something badly enough, and I worked hard, I would get it. Even when I was in the concentration camp, I knew that I would survive.

My father had to travel to the villages to visit his craftsmen and instead of paying someone to take him, he bought a car, a Ford Model T. My father learned how to drive but never passed his driving test. During his final driving test, with the inspector sitting next to him, he was asked for the time. My father took his hand off the wheel to get his pocket watch and in doing so he fell for the inspector's trick and failed the test. He still advertised that he had a car and charged people to travel with him to the villages. Every morning three or four people would accompany him. My mother benefited from my father's new arrangement too as she received perfume from one of his customers who was a perfumer.

Once, my father called me into his room and removed a little book from a drawer to show me the money he had saved for my dowry. He told me the dowry was for when I got married. I was outraged and told him that someone should have to pay *him* to have me as a bride.

My parents belonged to an orthodox synagogue, kept a kosher home, observed the Sabbath (there was always a *Cholent*), and went to the synagogue on the high holidays. My mother would dress in a gray wool suit with a silver fox shawl for Passover and Hanukkah and her hats were specifically designed with open tops so her blond hair was always visible. She was quite tall and pretty and people would stare at her when she walked into the synagogue. My mother had a large family and we always had company. Relatives would stay with us for about two weeks on their way to the United States.

I spent my days going to an elite school, *Realgymnasium*, and couldn't wait to leave it behind. Everything was taught in Hebrew and the teachers were all Jewish. Many students belonged to Zionist movements like *Hashomer Hazayir* and *Beitar*. The sports organization, Maccabee, helped students prepare for *Aliyah* to Israel.

For as long as I can remember, even though it was quite a distance, I would walk to school. Every morning, before we left for school, my mother would give my brother and I a glass of heavy cream and a Danish. It was so cold that when you walked out into the street your breath would freeze. Sometimes, when the weather was terrible, we would take a city bus to school. Although insignificant, I can recall the man who sat across from

9

me on the bus would constantly blink. By the time we got off, I was doing the same thing.

School was difficult. We were given a good deal of homework, and if you didn't pass a course, you would have to be tutored during the summer. I was an average student and only had difficulty understanding chemistry. In winter I was on the ice at the skating rink and in autumn and spring, I would spend my days at Maccabee. I loved ping-pong and became a ping-pong champion. Really, I was an athlete, not a scholar. My friends were plentiful and my life was wonderful.

Then, it was fashionable to be a communist in Lithuania. It was illegal, however, to have anything to do with Russia, but you could be a communist. My father's sister, Aunt Shifra, was a communist. Every year, on the first day of May, they would display their membership with the party by sending a pigeon with a red ribbon tied to it out their window. I used to love watching this. I had a friend who lived across from my aunt and when I would visit, my father would warn me against visiting my aunt because the communists would put me in jail.

My aunt, her husband, and her son fascinated me. You had to walk up to their, substandard, top floor apartment and I would sneak up there all the time. There were always men discussing the future of the world and Communism. They all seemed very intelligent and I was curious about their discussions. They often had wonderful food to eat that was completely different from the regular household food to which I was accustomed. Aunt Shifra's husband was a communist too and because he had a good job, they flourished in the years 1939 and 1940. When the Russians invaded Lithuania, the communists, including my aunt's family, thought they would be honored, but the Russians didn't want anything to do with them. When word of the impending German occupation reached them through the Underground, my aunt, uncle, and cousin left for Russia.

My grandfather on my mother's side, was a wonderful man. After my grandmother's death, he married her sister, as was customary in those days. He was a very good-looking man with a small, well-maintained beard who always dressed beautifully in a vest with a gold watch attached to it. He and his wife lived in a small town and I remember they had a lovely backyard with a big barn in it. I used to love that mysterious barn, full of beautiful things, a small wagon, and copper dishes. My mother also had two brothers and a sister, who sadly died at a young age before the war. My mother's family were all tall, blond, and good looking.

One of my uncles, Rachmeal, lived in Kibart, a small town on the Lithuanian-German border. He was married to Rosa, who came from a substantially wealthy family in Libau, Latvia. They weren't young when they married, probably around 25 or 26 years old. Uncle Rachmeal had a good job, was smart and spoke German like a German.

Uncle Rachmeal and Rosa had a large apartment in an affluent part of Kibart. I spent some time there during school holidays and loved being with them. I can't recall why, but they used to put grapefruits on the windowsills. They loved the fresh air and kept the apartment windows open all year round – it was so cold that they would put a hot water bottle in my bed to help keep me warm in winter. Aunt Rosa was determined to learn English and would go to a teacher in Germany for lessons. I remember going with her and, while waiting for her to finish, would marvel at the magnificently large parlor with couches and a Persian rug.

Uncle Heshel, my mother's second brother, actually ended up marrying a girl I knew from school, though the marriage was the result of a well-thought-out plan she devised herself. She was infatuated with my uncle and was determined that they were meant to be together. When my uncle was 27 years old, he went to Polanga, a resort where young people vacationed. She found out his room number and rented the room next door. All the rooms had balconies and her balcony was next to his. She waited for him to go out onto his balcony and when he did, she walked out onto hers but without a top on. That did it. He married her.

Her name was Lena and she was an interesting young woman. She was tall and blond, much like the rest of the family. They had to wait a year to get married because she was still in high school but after they did, they rented a nice apartment facing the Yemen River and invited me to visit them. I went to visit them one day and I arrived at around 11 o'clock but as Lena answered the door in an alluring white nightgown, I could see that they weren't expecting me. When I looked into the bedroom, I saw that the bedding was black. I ran out in shock after seeing this. My uncle asked me to come back and told me Lena liked the black bedding and that there was nothing wrong with it. But, in my young mind, it was unsettling.

They had a child but we lost contact with them when we were forced into the ghetto. I later found out that Uncle Heshel and their child were killed. After the war, I met Lena in a café in Paris, she was diabetic but was eating ice cream and cake. I asked her if eating the sugared food was the best thing for her, and she responded saying that she no longer cared.

During the summer we went to the country. We usually took a boat to Kolotova, a beautiful resort town on the Niemunas River, about 30 kilometers west of Kovno. Once, because my mother was experiencing pain in her legs, possibly arthritis, we went to a popular spa in Biershtan. We rented a cottage for the whole summer and my father would join us for the weekends, arriving on Friday nights with a big bag of bagels. My mother would enjoy the mud baths and the natural springs. We would go swimming and ride bicycles and we seldomly went to restaurants because my mother liked to cook. If we did eat out, she would insist that we finish everything on our plates because many starving people couldn't afford to eat at restaurants.

III. THE RUSSIAN INVASION

*"It is well known that the Soviet Union closely regulates all
organizations and movements,
including religion."*
Billy Graham

My idyllic life changed on June 16, 1940, when the Russians invaded Lithuania. In addition to limiting the Jews' freedom of movement, they punished Lithuanians who they believed had helped the Germans. Initially, people were happy the Russians had arrived and greeted them with parades and flowers but the Russians gradually changed our way of life. All free institutions and Jewish communal organizations were eliminated, Hebrew was banned and properties of many Jewish people were confiscated.

The Russians nationalized factories and privately owned stores, and in doing so, increased the price of goods because of supply shortages. This was a harsh blow to the economy, felt especially by the middle class, which was mainly Jewish. They introduced

14

Russian history and language in all schools and universities, we had to sing the Russian national anthem and they indoctrinated us in the history of the Bolsheviks.

On June 14, 1941, the Soviet secret police carried out large scale arrests and deportations. Seven thousand Jews were among the tens of thousands of Lithuanians sent to Siberia for internment in labor camps, not because of their religion, but because they were capitalists. Although these Jews struggled under harsh conditions, they were fortunate to have escaped the torture and killings of the impending German invasion.

We feared being sent to Siberia because of my father's affiliation with Germany, but we were yet to understand the horrors in store for us at the hands of the Germans. In the autumn of 1940, over 80 percent of the enterprises confiscated in Lithuania belonged to Jews. For those who had businesses taken away from them, life got easier. Before the Russians occupied Lithuania, success was measured by how prosperous one's family was in business. After the Russians came, and no longer concerned for the businesses that had been confiscated, we were forced to prosper elsewhere, so many concentrated on excelling in school – to create a better life.

There were, however, some advantages to the Russians' arrival. The Russians abolished antisemitic laws. For the first time, higher education was made available to both male and female Jewish students. Jewish people could work in government and party offices. Many Jews were allowed to serve in state ministries and could be court judges. Before the Russians arrived, these laws weren't recognized and this confirmed the Lithuanians belief that the Russian presence was powered by the Jews.

A resistance group called "The Lithuanian Activist Front" (LAF) was formed in Kovno which grew to 35,000 members. They referred to themselves as 'partisans' and were called 'White Ribbons' by others because they wore white ribbons wrapped around their left arms. The LAF disseminated antisemitic literature and blamed the Jews for the Russian occupation.

The horror stories of what the Germans were doing to the Jews started to reach us. Our relatives in Germany, who were shopkeepers, wrote to us asking for our help to escape. The Germans had taken the head of the family and said he would return in a few days. The Germans came back the next day with a box that contained the man's remains. My father helped bring the rest of the family to Kovno. We couldn't imagine that people were capable of doing these things, but the escapees from Poland told us about the German atrocities.

My parents knew that something was very wrong and began planning an escape from Lithuania, but it was too late and they were concerned about our ability to survive if something happened to my father. So, my father went to see his family in Vilna and took a beautiful grey, fur-collared, woolen coat with him. When he returned with the coat, the lining had been removed and replaced with mink skins. He believed, if something happened to him, I could sell the coat for survival.

IV. THE GERMAN INVASION

"There's a long road of suffering ahead of you. But don't lose courage. You've already escaped the gravest danger: selection. So now, muster your strength, and don't lose heart. We shall all see the day of liberation. Have faith in life. Above all else, have faith. Drive out despair, and you will keep death away from yourselves. Hell is not for eternity. And now, a prayer – or rather, a piece of advice: let there be comradeship among you. We are all brothers, and we are all suffering the same fate. The same smoke floats over all our heads. Help one another. It is the only way to survive."

Elie Wiesel, *Night*

On June 21, 1941, on my way to school to collect my high school diploma, a bomb exploded nearby. I fell on the sidewalk and tore the silk stockings my mother had saved for me to wear that day. I was so upset about the torn stockings and in shock from the bomb blast that I forgot about collecting my diploma and ran home. My father said, "The Germans made it after all. They are here!" I didn't understand the hell we were about to go through, yet.

The German invasion gave the Lithuanians motivation to ruthlessly attack Jews. SS Major Stahlecker offered help to partisan gangs who eradicated the Jews. The LAF leaped into action and by noon on June 23, 1941, they had taken control of the telegraph and telephone center, the central post office, police headquarters, arsenals, and the radio station in Kovno. They had organized armed Lithuanian units known as *Schutzmannschaft*.

The journalist Klimatis led a 300-strong unit. These units helped the Germans in the persecution and killing of Jews. They worked with the *Einsatzgruppen*, a German paramilitary unit whose purpose was to eliminate Jews. On June 25, 1941, 1,500 Jews were killed and the next night, 2,300 were killed. Before the German invasion, there were 35,000 Jews in Kovno, but by the end of October 1941, only half were left.

Hundreds of Lithuanians tried leaving Kovno with the fleeing Russians, but they didn't get far. The Germans killed people at train stations and were strafing the roads. Some made it to Russia but were turned away at the border. Those who returned to Kovno were unable to get back into their homes.

The partisan gangs went from house to house, killing, looting, and raping Jews, using the excuse that the Jews had helped the Russians and therefore should be punished. These stories, although abound with the atrocities committed, also demonstrate some people's kindness.

Once, the partisans had broken into my husband's apartment, before we knew each other, and he warned them against attacking his family. As a lieutenant in the Lithuanian army, he wore a big medal identifying his rank. They laughed at his warning, slapped him around, and relieved him of his medal. The Lithuanian janitor of the apartment building arrived, having heard the commotion, and told them to leave. Fortunately, they listened to the janitor and all were spared from further harm or a worse fate.

One cannot possibly imagine the confusion, terror, and despair after the Germans marched into Kovno. The Russians, who had occupied the area for two years, deserted the city. They fled by truck, foot, and any other way available. With the sudden disappearance of the Russians, the prisons were left unguarded and the Lithuanian partisans freed all the prisoners.

There was chaos in the streets and the Lithuanians had turned into animals. People we had dealt with for years suddenly turned against us. They were like a frenzied mob being held back by barriers and once those barriers were removed, they attacked. It was impossible to find places to hide and there was no way to protect ourselves against the horde of rabid Lithuanians. We watched as those who resisted were murdered right in front of us. We prayed for survival.

People criticized us for not defending ourselves against the Germans and Lithuanians but we had no choice. We had nowhere to go – like animals cornered in a cage.

During the Czarist rule, a series of nine forts surrounding Kovno were built to protect the city from a German invasion. The forts were used to incarcerate criminals, but during the German invasion of Kovno, the forts were used to imprison, torture, and execute Jews. Twenty-five thousand Jews from Kovno, 15,000 Jews from Germany and Poland, and thousands of Russian prisoners were massacred at these forts.

During June and July of 1941, Lithuanian terrorists rampaged throughout the country. They made Fort VII into a concentration camp, where about 6,000 Jews from Kovno were killed using machine guns and hand grenades.

On June 24, 1941, the Lithuanians arrested and imprisoned Jewish men, women, and children without cause. They were beaten and thrown out of cells into corridors where Lithuanian clerks noted the identity of each person before the Jews were forced into a prison yard. There, under a reinforced guard of Lithuanian partisans, they were put onto red buses belonging to the city transport system and driven to Fort VII.

The Jews were crammed into long passageways at Fort VII and were killed in groups, only after being tortured and, often in a woman's case, raped. After one group was shot and killed, the next group would have to cover the corpses before being shot and killed themselves. The situation at Fort VII was unimaginable. Thousands of people were made to stand in the scorching heat without water. The killings were orchestrated by the Germans, but executed entirely by the Lithuanians.

Basketball was a major event in Lithuania, the Lithuanians were world champions and, at the time, basketball games between the Germans and the Lithuanians were played. When a team was victorious, each of the winning players was awarded ten Jews to shoot at Fort VII. One evening, a bus filled with the Lithuanian basketball team arrived at Fort VII. They got off the bus and chose 30 Jews, led them to an embankment where they killed them and then got back on the bus, singing.

Before the German invasion, the famous Slobodka *Yeshiva* housed well-known rabbis, rabbinical students, a cultural center, many Jewish institutions, and numerous synagogues connected with the Yeshiva. But, after the purge, a visitor to Slobodka found houses filled with blood, mutilated bodies, and in one house, a severed head on a table with needles in its eyes. He found a family of five, all choked to death in a house, and in another, a family of six nailed to a table.

Civilians and German soldiers looking at the
massacre of 68 Jews in the Lietukis garage of
Kaunas (Lithuania) on June 25 or 27, 1941
(Wikipedia, Source: Zentrale Stelle der
Landesjustizverwaltungen, Ludwigsburg; DÖW,
Vienna)

The massacre of Jews at the Lietukis garage occurred on June 25, 1941. A group of about 70 Jewish men was made to clean the garage floor, which was covered with horse manure, with their bare hands while Lithuanians and German soldiers watched. When the Jewish men were told to wash, some Lithuanians assaulted the Jews with sticks, rifle butts, crowbars, and other garage tools. The Jews, writhing in pain, collapsed on the pavement. They were then dragged across the garage floor and hosed with water until they were revived. The Lithuanians would then repeat these heinous activities until they all died.

The man who killed the most Jews, known as the 'Death Dealer', put his crowbar to one side, fetched an accordion, stood on the mound of corpses, and played the Lithuanian National Anthem. Others joined in singing and clapping to the anthem as women held their children up to better observe the disturbance.

It was later told that the parents of the 'Death Dealer' had been kidnapped from their beds two days earlier. They were suspected nationalists, and for this, they were shot and killed. The 'Death Dealer's' involvement in the massacre was his revenge. There were many Germans present but they didn't interfere. A photographer, serving in the German army, took pictures that were turned into the German authorities.

Kovno - Lithuanian 'Death Dealer' at Lietukis Garage, 1941 (Bundesarchiv)

On June 26, 1941, the Lithuanian partisans, with the blessing of the German authorities, went into Slobodka, the religious area of Kovno, and murdered all the rabbinical students and destroyed all the Torah scrolls. They went from house to house stabbing and killing men, women, children, and the elderly. They severed limbs and decapitated heads. They chased families out of their beds and lined them up against walls and brutally shot them. As if this wasn't enough, the Lithuanians decided the public should witness their deeds. Gathering about 30 Jewish men and transporting them to the banks of the Vilia River, the partisans shot and killed them in front of a, cheering and applauding, Lithuanian audience. They had already prepared a pit for the men to be buried in. Three thousand eight hundred Jews were killed during the two-night slaughter. They made Jews remove the dead bodies from the streets and bury them elsewhere.

Karl Jäger, the Commander of the Security Police and the *SD Einsatzkommando*, meticulously cataloged the Jewish deaths in what is now known as the 'Jäger Report'. In his report of the complete list of executions carried out in the Einsatzkommando 3 (EK3) area until December 1, 1941, Jäger notes that security police duties in Lithuania were taken over by the EK3 on July 2, 1941.

Upon his order, the following executions of Jews were conducted by Lithuanian partisans in Kovno (Kauen):

- *July 4, 1941 Kauen Fort VII 416 Jews, 47 Jewesses*
- *July 6, 1941 Kauen Fort VII2, 514 Jews*

The following actions were conducted in cooperation with Lithuanian partisans:

- *July 9, 1941 Kauen Fort VII21 Jews, 3 Jewesses*
- *July 19, 1941 Kauen Fort VII 17 Jews, 2 Jewesses*
- *Aug. 2, 1941 Kauen Fort IV 170 Jews, 1 US Jew, 1 US Jewess, 33 Jewesses*
- *August 9, 1941 Kauen Fort IV 484 Jews, 50 Jewesses*
- *August 18, 1941 Kauen Fort IV 639 Jews, 402 Jewesses, 711 Jewish intellectuals from ghetto in reprisal for sabotage action*
- *September 26, 1941 Kauen Fort IV412 Jews, 615 Jewesses, 581 Jewish children (sick and suspected epidemic cases)*

- *October 4, 1941 Kauen Fort IX 315 Jews, 712 Jewesses, 818 Jewish children (reprisal after German police officer shot in ghetto)*
- *October 29, 1941 Kauen Fort IX 2,007 Jews, 2,920 Jewesses, 4,273 Jewish children (mopping up ghetto of superfluous Jews)*
- *November 25, 1941 Kauen Fort IX 1,159 Jews 1,600 Jewesses, 175 Jewish children (resettlers from Berlin, Munich, and Frankfurt am Main)*
- *November 29, 1941 Kauen Fort IX 693 Jews, 1,155 Jewesses, 152 Jewish children (resettlers from Vienna and Breslau)*
- *November 29, 1941 Kauen Fort IX 17 Jews, 1 Jewess, for contravention of ghetto law, 1 Reichs German who converted to Jewish faith and attended rabbinical school*

Jäger concludes his report by stating that their objective – to solve the Jewish problem for Lithuania – had been achieved by EK3. The only Jews left were 15,000 workers and their families. These workers would be eliminated when no longer needed. He recommended that the men be sterilized and if Jewish women became pregnant they would be eliminated.[1]

---

1. Klee, Ernst, Dressen, Willi & Riess, Volker eds, *The Good Old Days*, Konecky & Konecky, 1988, p. 46 ff

V. THE GHETTO

"They dug the bodies out of the ground. They put their bare hands not only into death, not only into the syrups and bacteria of the body, but into emotions, beliefs, confessions. One man's memories then another's, thousands whose lives it was their duty to imagine...."
Anne Michaels

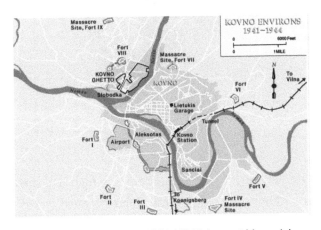

Kovno environs, 1941-1944. US Holocaust Memorial Museum.

In his book, *The Kovno Ghetto Diary*, Abraham Tory recants the events that occurred after the Lithuanian purge. The Germans ordered three Jewish leaders and two rabbis to meet at Gestapo headquarters and proposed that in order to stop the Lithuanian slaughter of Jews, they must move into a ghetto. They were told that the present situation of total disorder and unrest couldn't continue.

The Lithuanians wanted the Jews to move to a ghetto so they would no longer have anything to do with them. The Jews were given a choice; continue living amid the killings and rapes or move into a ghetto. The Germans also promised to release 3,000 women and children prisoners and to stop the slaughtering of Jews if they complied. After consulting with Lithuanian authorities, who refused to intervene, the Jews decided they had no choice but to recommend the move to the ghetto. The Jews had to make this move by August 15, 1941.

George Kadish. *Moving into the Kovno ghetto.* 1941. US Holocaust Memorial Museum Hidden History of the Kovno Ghetto.

I cannot remember moving to Slobodka, which had now become the ghetto. I know we didn't walk there because it was quite far from where we lived, across the Yemen River, and we didn't own a car. The ghetto dominated most of Slobodka and barbed wire fence had been erected around it. The 30,000 Jews who had survived the Lithuanian slaughters moved into this neighborhood that formerly housed only 7,000 people.

When I was in the United States Holocaust Memorial Museum, in Washington, there was a large poster, on one of the walls, of four people moving into the Slobodka ghetto. I realized, on closer inspection, that is was me and my family in the poster. My mother, father, brother, and me. I told the museum curator this, and although they searched everywhere in the archives, they couldn't find the original photograph or remember where it came from.

Two sections made up the ghetto: the small ghetto and the large ghetto, divided by Paneriu Street. Barbed wire fencing surrounded each section, but as Paneriu Street was not part of the ghettos, it had no wire fencing. The two ghettos were linked by a wooden bridge, built by the Jews, that could be blocked by the Germans at will. At first, my family and I lived in the small ghetto and we were assigned an apartment that formerly belonged to Lithuanians. I don't know what happened to the previous owners of the apartment but I assume the Germans had forced them out. We had some furniture, although I cannot recall where the furniture came from. The ghetto could have passed as a small town in a western movie: run-down wooden houses, unpaved streets, no streetlights, and a few stores.

A series of orders from the mayor, who was also the military commander of Kovno, were issued. One order prohibited Jews, who escaped from Kovno at the time the Russians were fleeing, from returning and another order was punishing those who had helped them. Orders demanded that Jews were only allowed in

27

public places between 6 a.m. and 8 p.m. and had to wear the yellow Star of David, on the left breast, at all times. The practice of keeping Jews in ghettos and having them wear the Star of David was first introduced by the Lithuanians but became a practice the Germans continued elsewhere.

Orders were published daily. Jews were forbidden to walk on sidewalks and had to walk, single file, along the right side of the road. We couldn't enter promenade walks and public parks or use benches. The use of public transportation such as buses, taxis, and horse carriages was also prohibited.

Gloom and despair covered the ghetto like a heavy blanket. Not daring to go out, we stayed at home most days and in order to survive, we traded our gold, silver, and other valuable items to farmers for food. Pillows or extra clothes were no longer important, and the farmers were glad to acquire the gold or silver.

Photographer unknown. *The Kovno Ghetto Jewish Council*. 1943. Yad Vashem Photo Archives. Order of appearance from left to right: Avraham Tory (secretary), Leib Garfunkel (Deputy Chair), Dr. Elkhnanan Elkes (Chair), Yakov Goldberg (Labor Office Head), Zvi Levin (Underground Link).

The Germans told the Jews that they had to form a Council, called the *Ältestenrat*, to manage the affairs of the ghetto. They had to elect a Chief Jew, or *Oberjude*, to head the Ältestenrat. On August 4, 1941, the Jewish leaders met with and convinced Dr. Elkhanan Elkes, a physician and head of the Jewish hospital in Kovno, to become the Oberjude. Dr. Elkes was known for his outstanding moral values, courage, integrity, dedication to Jewish causes, involvement in Jewish life and culture, Zionist causes, and assistance with the Anti-Nazi Underground. He also spoke fluent German, which helped with communication with the Germans.

The Ältestenrat formed its own police force and appointed Michael Kopelman, a well-respected businessman, as the chief of police. Because Kopelman had no police experience, they also appointed Michael Bramson, a former high school teacher, and army veteran, as deputy chief to run the day-to-day affairs of the force. Kopelman and Bramson managed to recruit from all areas of the ghetto and by November 1942, the force numbered 150 men.

On August 19, 1941, both the Germans and Lithuanians crowded the ghetto streets. They went from house to house, taking what they wanted, and beating the inhabitants mercilessly. They were ordered to kill a certain number of Jews each day to scare the remaining Jews into relinquishing their valuables. On September 1, six Jews were killed, and the next day, six more were killed in their sleep. Three more Jews were shot and killed each day for the following three days.

The Germans promised to stop the searches, and killings if the Jews voluntarily gave up their valuables. The Ältestenrat issued an order for the ghetto's inhabitants to hand in all their valuables the next day and most complied. The Germans were devious in their schemes to intimidate us.

The Ältestenrat was charged with finding housing for the Jewish population but many families, for whom housing couldn't be found, lived in deserted pigsties, public buildings or schools, and had no kitchens, furniture, or running water.

Attending school was deemed illegal by the Germans so makeshift schools were set up in houses for about ten students at a time. Food was brought from the outside. There was one Jewish bakery and one butchery and once a week, Jewish musicians would perform on the shores of the river. People would go to the river to swim and bathe as there was only one public bath in town and most of the houses didn't have running water.

Our stay in the small ghetto was short because the Germans slowly started emptying the small ghetto out not long after we relocated there. The Germans would come into the ghetto, with a horn blaring, calling various groups of Jewish people out into the street. These were called 'Aktions.' These Aktions began on August 18, 1941, when the Jewish Council was ordered to provide 500 educated Jewish men to work in the Kovno City archives. The promise of a good job, food, and money encouraged 534 men to volunteer. This promise was never fulfilled and those brilliant young men were never heard from again. It's thought that they were taken to Fort IV and murdered there. Sometime later, Jews working at Fort IV found execution orders of the 500 men, indicating that 50 pounds of sugar had been sabotaged by them. For every pound of sugar that had been damaged, ten men were killed. The Germans consequently destroyed the Jewish elite.

When Lithuania gained independence in 1924, Fort IX served as a city prison. When the last fort was constructed, it was considered an innovative solution, the walls were made of concrete with the thickness of the ceiling reaching up to two meters. Fort IX had secure hidden tunnels that served as evacuation routes and connected it to the other forts.

After the second Soviet occupation, from 1940, the bloody history of Fort IX began. During the occupation, the fort was used as a transfer point for prisoners of the NKVD (People's

Commissariat of Internal Affairs), mainly former independent Lithuanian politicians, to the Gulag forced labor camps, located primarily in Siberia. When the Germans took power in Lithuania, Fort IX served as a place for mass killings of Jewish people.

The horrors of Auschwitz and the other German death camps have been embedded in our minds since the end of World War II, but few have learned about the horrors of Fort VII and Fort IX, in Kovno. Instead of gas chambers, the Germans murdered Kovno Jews by torture, beatings, shootings, and burying them alive at the Forts.

The Aktions that took place in the ghetto would result in a 'Death March' that took the Jews on a road, three or four kilometers long, uphill from the ghetto to Fort IX. The Germans called it *Der Weg zum Himmelfahrt* ('The Way to Heaven').

"Before their execution, the detainees were incarcerated in underground cells known as 'casements' in damp, darkness, and fear. There, people fought with one another for a brighter corner in the cells, for a piece of a straw mattress, for a scrap of food, or for a crumb of bread. There, Jews were shackled in iron chains, harnessed to ploughs in place of horses, forced to dig into peat-pits inside the fort, and often whipped to death. There, one soon lost one's human image and one's own will – there, life turned into senseless pain, after which death came as redemption."[1]

One man from Kovno, who had been a prisoner at Fort IX, escaped after five months and told us about the massacres at the fort. The Germans separated the Jewish-Russian prisoners from the other Russian prisoners and murdered them with the Jews from Kovno.

On September 15, 1941, German SA Captain Jordan, the *Sturmführer* in charge of the ghetto, issued 5,000 certificates, later known as Jordan certificates or life papers, and instructed the Council to distribute them to one artisan or trade specialist in each family. The Council members were suspicious and feared these certificates were another way to separate and murder the Jews.

On October 4, after watching an Aktion, in which Jews with Jordan certificates weren't removed, it became clear that those who didn't have a certificate would be killed. The Council was besieged with people begging for certificates, an unruly mob eventually broke down the door of the Council building and ransacked it in search of Jordan certificates.

Photographer unknown. *Jewish Forced Laborers Making Shoes.* 1943. US Holocaust Memorial Museum.

The Ältestenrat realized the importance of jobs and as long as the Germans needed workers, lives were being saved. Jobs increased food rations and allowed contact with others who could smuggle in food and other much needed supplies. One Council member persuaded SA Captain Jordan of the need to set up workshops in the ghetto. The workshops, including a tailor shop, shoemaker, milliner, furrier, a glove maker, and shoe repair, provided work for many, especially those too weak to walk to work outside the ghetto.

The first project assigned to the workshops was to fix thousands of pieces of clothing, robbed from the Jews during the early house searches. Later, the Germans used the workshops to mend army clothing.

Furniture and toy workshops were established, and the Germans could obtain gifts and furniture from them. The workers were able to smuggle out supplies to help ghetto families and when groups of Jewish fighters left the ghetto to join the resistance, they brought warm clothing, boots, and equipment back with them. They were also able to smuggle children out with supply wagons leaving the ghetto, hiding them in the workshops during Aktions or deportations.

The mapmaker, William Mishell, created a graphics department and was able to provide all the notices given by the Germans. Daily orders were posted instructing us to turn over our electrical appliances, property papers, money exceeding 100 rubles per family, gold, silver, and furs.

On October 4, 1941, the 'Hospital for Contagious Diseases' Aktion happened. Healthy residents from the small ghetto, which had now been closed down, went to the hospital hoping to find shelter. The Germans, having, allegedly, been informed that a patient in the hospital had leprosy, forced all personal, including the hospital watchman and his son, into the hospital.

The hospital gates were locked, the doors sealed and the hospital was set alight with everyone – doctors, nurses and patients – trapped inside. Firemen were ordered not to intervene. In addition to the lives lost, all medical equipment, records, and medicine were destroyed. There are no words to describe this horror. Only monsters could do such a thing. From that day, doctors kept all the diseases in the ghetto a secret.

---

1. Tory, Avraham, *Surviving the Holocaust: The Kovno Ghetto Diary*, Harvard University Press, 1990, p. 508

VI. THE GREAT AKTION

How can I fall asleep if execution
awaits me? How can I doze
in the lion's paw? Therefore, I lie
with eyes open, conversing with my heart.
When will the hangman's hand smite me
will it happen on a glorious night
when the nightingale pours out its song
and herbs perfume the air?
On that luminous night we'll be led
to slaughter sounds of weeping tearing
the heart; only the baby will be happy:
oh, we're going out for a stroll
Or will it be summer's end-air
overflowing with the land's blessings
when the executioner decides to do us in?
Or will it be on a stark autumn's night
rain, cold as needle punctures
drizzling down our cheeks

when we're all led to be butchered?
Or will it be in the midst of a grim
winter-the storm bursting into the house
making treasures of snow dance
and the cold freezing the spine.
K.L. Yemo (Moshe Klein), *Nightmares*

On October 25, 1941, Master Sergeant Rauca and Captain Schmitz met with the Council, informing them that the size of the workforce needed to increase and that workers with jobs that were more physically demanding needed more nourishment. In order to provide more food for them and their families, the Germans needed to separate them from workers with jobs that required no physical activity. Those with less-active jobs would be moved to the small ghetto and physical workers would be provided with better living arrangements.

The Council was asked to send out a notice telling the Jews to report to Demokratu Square at 6 a.m. on October 28, for living reassignment.

We were to leave our apartments open and anyone found in an apartment would be shot. The Council members didn't trust Rauca and were concerned. There were constant rumors of ditches being dug at the Fort IX. Every time ditches were dug, it was followed by an Aktion. The Council members consulted Chief Rabbi Shapiro and, after considering the dilemma, advised the Council to send out the notice to save as many lives as possible.

The Council issued the order and the reaction was varied. Some stayed home and prayed while others feasted on their food supply and invited others to drink and eat so as not to leave anything for the Germans. Many hid money and valuables under floorboards or buried in pits in their courtyards and single women looked for men to act as their husbands.

On a rainy Tuesday, under the pretense of a roll call to reassign housing, 30,000 beleaguered Jews, left their homes and reported to Demokratu Square.

It's difficult to fathom the enormity of this operation, the sight of thousands of men, women, children, old and young, strong and weak, near-death and dying. It was as if hell had opened its gates and welcomed the masses. We walked with heavy hearts and held up those too weak to proceed on their own. Many brought documents showing employment by one of the ghetto institutions in the hopes that this would save them. While we assembled, armed Lithuanian partisans raided the ghetto houses and searched for any Jews who may have been hiding.

The square was the size of a football field and we were lined up in rows, the head of each family standing at the front. The Council members were first, then the Jewish policemen and their families. The workers of the ghetto institutions, Jewish labor crews, and their families came next.

After waiting for three hours, the Gestapo entourage finally arrived. Captain Schmitz, the Gestapo Deputy Chief, Master Sergeant Rauca, Captain Jordan, and Captain Tornbaum were among them. They were accompanied by a squad of Lithuanian partisans and German policemen. Master Sergeant Rauca stood at the front and waved people over, either to his right or his left, simply with one finger. He waved the Council members and Jewish police, with their families, to his left. It fast became apparent that to be on his left meant you would live. He sent members of the Jewish labor teams and workers employed at a

German military installation, together with their families, to his left too.

Rauca carried on with his selection, barely pausing while feasting on a sandwich, wrapped in wax paper, and enjoying a cigarette. This heartless man was deaf to the cries and pleadings of those before him.

My family and I were lined up next to my best friend and her family – eight of us in a row. With a flick of his finger, Rauca had sent her family to his right, and us to his left. Why? Why were they sent to be killed while we were allowed to live? We were all healthy people but they didn't look at faces. They just knew that four should go here and four should go there. I realized then that there was no hope. Survival was determined by sheer luck.

The Jewish police helped as many as they could. They quietly moved people from the right side to the left. They tried to comfort others and aided those who fell to the ground so they wouldn't be shot.

Those who were sent to the right were relocated to the small ghetto. Some thought that they would stay there and began looking for deserted houses to fix up and live in. They even negotiated the formation of a Council, similar to the one in the big ghetto. But, early one morning, Germans and drunken Lithuanian partisans broke into their houses and ordered them out and to assemble. It was clear to everybody, too late, what was about to happen.

What a sight… Thousands of people marching to what they knew was their death. Those in the big ghetto watched as their friends and relatives were herded along *Der Weg zum Himmelfahrt*. Some tried to escape but were shot while running, their bodies strewn in the fields. When they got to Fort IX, their clothes were taken and they were thrown into ditches, 300 at a time. The children were first, followed by the women and finally, the men. Some were shot first, but the vast majority were thrown in alive. They were screaming and crying, but the Germans' ears were closed to the Jewish cries.

After the killing, one Lithuanian described how he stabbed small children with his bayonet and threw them into the pits, half alive. He didn't bother stabbing the smallest children, it was too much work. Ten thousand Jews were murdered in that Aktion.

There were a few survivors. One, a 12-year-old boy who managed to get back to the ghetto, described his experience and the horror spread throughout the ghetto, like an unquenched fire. Very little hope remained, there was no one to count on for help, only good fortune would keep the remaining few alive.

We knew that this was the beginning of a descent into hell. Now that I am older and wiser, I realize that one cannot change destiny. My destiny was to survive hell and meet my wonderful husband. Perhaps I never would have met him, were we not thrown into the inferno together.

The crimes the Germans committed were so unspeakable that to think of them as humans would literally drive you mad, the alternative was to think of them as creatures from hell and to try our best to survive. I won't dwell on the past and I cannot allow myself to hate – it's self-destructive. But I will never forgive the Germans or forget what they did.

My brother was tall, blond, and spoke perfect Lithuanian. He used to sneak out during his workday and just blend in with the Lithuanians. He was well connected and managed to leave the ghetto on and off to bring us food. When he was 14 years old, he would sneak out to meet his Lithuanian friends, tearing off the yellow Star of David to do so. My mother managed to smuggle our sterling silverware into the ghetto and would give him one piece at a time to barter for food so we didn't starve.

When the small ghetto was closed, we relocated to the big ghetto. A little house was assigned to us, it had a kitchen and two bedrooms. My Aunt Rosa, Uncle Rachmeal's wife, and her two-year-old came to live with us. Uncle Rachmeal was taken in the first Aktion and never came back. My other uncle, Heshel, lived in the ghetto with his wife Lena and their small child. Lena survived the war, but my uncle and their child were killed. No details were given about their deaths but I assume they met the same fate as Rachmeal.

Daily life in the ghetto rarely differed. You could say that we lived in a 'gated community'. Every day we would wake up, leave through the gate, and go to work, mostly for the Germans. Dr. Elkes was a friend of my husband's father – they went to yeshiva together.

Before our marriage, my husband would always be assigned to good jobs through a beneficial relationship with Dr. Elkes. My husband had experience in construction so he was assigned to public works. His job was to ensure the roads allowed the Germans to transport Jews to Fort IX. When that project was complete, he was assigned as leader of a crew that would transport lumber from ships to lumber mills.

His job, just before we were married, was to assign people to ongoing projects. People would gather every morning in a big lot, and he would assign them to jobs. When we first met, he was told to pick 20 people to work with him. I happened to be standing there and he picked me along with 19 other girls. He liked me as soon as he saw me and made me his secretary.

My secretarial job consisted of measuring a pound of flour into bags that would be given to the workers at the end of the day. On the first day, I didn't measure the flour correctly and had nothing left for myself. He told me that, next time, I should measure some out for myself first.

Once, a group of young women, including myself, were taken to a farm in the country to pick vegetables. A German came galloping toward us on a saddled horse. He asked me if I had ever ridden a horse and when I replied that I had not, he said it was about time that I learned.

He removed the saddle and made me mount the horse which immediately took off at full speed, I barely managed to hold on. On my return, I dismounted and was told to pick vegetables again. He probably thought I would fall off and get killed. I guess I was his entertainment for the morning. I don't think they saw us as human. We couldn't look them in the eye and risk being killed and they didn't want to touch us, thank goodness – we would have been raped otherwise.

My husband, Raphael (Ralph), had a nice apartment and would often host parties. They had plenty bottles of vodka and would drink, listen to music, and have a good time. He was six years older than me and I was not yet a part of this scene. Before we married, he invited me to one of his parties and sent a mutual friend to escort me.

It was dark when I arrived and I also arrived later than the others, who were already drinking. I felt uncomfortable, being the youngest person there, watching them drink. I asked my friend to take me home, but Ralph insisted that I stay and dance with him but when I refused, he told our friend to take me home. We began courting after that night. My father knew his family and liked the fact that he was older. Family is very important in Europe. Sometime later Ralph asked my father for his blessing to marry me, my father knew that Ralph would take care of me and he consented.

We were married in a barber's tent by Joseph Malnik, a Justice of the Peace, in 1943. My mother hosted a wedding reception and my brother managed to barter for a turkey that my mother cooked, like a Cholent. She stored it in the bakery, covered with paper, on a Friday evening but on Saturday evening, when she went to pick it up, she discovered the turkey had been stolen. I felt so sorry for her, it was difficult to get the ingredients and she had worked so hard on it. We did, however, have many bottles of vodka so the wedding dinner was a huge success and a good time was had by all.

I moved into my husband's apartment after our wedding. The family all slept in one room. My husband and I shared a bunk bed with my sister-in-law and brother-in-law, us on the top, and them on the bottom and my mother-in-law slept on a separate bed.

As newly-weds, we had no privacy but it didn't seem to bother us. Ralph's brother, Misha, was involved with the Underground. He didn't look Jewish, so he was able to leave the ghetto and go to Lithuanian organizations as a spy for the Underground. He would copy maps of where German installations were located and relay other important information to the Underground.

Once, Misha was coming back to the ghetto but was caught by a German soldier. He was beaten and put in jail but managed to escape and return home. Understandably, the Underground was very secretive. Members were divided into groups of five and had no knowledge of other groups or who was in them – they only knew their own. Talking about the Underground was also strictly prohibited and if caught, could get you killed by the Underground itself. One of the leaders of the Underground was the gifted Yiddish poet and writer, Chaim Yellin (1912-1944).

Portrait of Chaim Yellin. January 1944. Yad Vashem Photo Archives.

Chaim Yellin tried to escape when the Germans invaded but was caught and sent to live in the Kovno ghetto. He was wanted by the Germans so he rarely went outside, if he did, he always had a bandage covering his face, appearing as though he was suffering from toothache. He and his fellow fighters acquired arms, developed secret training areas in the ghetto and established contact with Soviet partisans in the forests surrounding Kovno.

In the summer of 1943, Yellin helped merge communist and Zionist partisans into one united resistance organization, The General Jewish Fighting Organization (*Yidishe Algemeyne Kamfs Organizatsye* or the JFO). The JFO had 600 members and united the major resistance groups in the ghetto. About 300 ghetto fighters escaped, joining Soviet partisan groups in the forests. Yellin was, unfortunately, captured by the Germans while on a mission outside the ghetto. He was tortured and killed in May 1944.

Photographer unknown. *Group Portrait of Jewish Lithuanian Partisan Unit.* 1944. US Holocaust Memorial Museum, courtesy of Eliezer Zilberis.

VII. ESCAPE FROM FORT IX

"'Hope' is the thing with feathers –
that perches in the soul –
and sings the tune without the words –
and never stops at all."
Emily Dickinson

In August 1943, orders came from Berlin that any evidence of the mass graves at Fort IX needed to be destroyed by the end of January 1944. Seventy-five prisoners were selected to carry out the order but 11 of them were too ill to work so they were shot and killed and the remaining 64 were put to work. The group mainly consisted of Jewish men, but there were four Jewish women, and one non-Jewish, Polish woman. In his book, *The Kovno Ghetto Diary*, Avraham Tory describes the gruesome work performed by these 64 prisoners.

The 64-member team was divided into four separate units. The first unit, called the 'diggers', were charged with scraping the top layer of dirt off the graves and removing the first layer of corpses.

After that, they used ladders to descend into the pit and, with pitchforks, tossed the remaining corpses to the surface. A search for valuables was conducted, gold teeth and jewelry were removed and, once polished, were turned over to the German supervisors. The corpses were naked.

Most of the Lithuanian Jews had no bullet holes, and from the expression on their faces, it was surmised that they were buried alive. Some of the prisoners working recognized relatives and friends. In one instance, a digger recognized his brother.

The second unit, called 'porters', were required to count the bodies in the presence of a supervisor and pile them on wooden pallets to be transported to the pyre.

At the pyre, the third unit, called the 'firemen', went to work. Every 24 hours they prepared the corpses by piling them in layers on logs under the supervision of the *Brandmeister*, an expert in burning. They had to burn 300 corpses a day. The corpses were set alight, layer by layer, and their ashes were either buried or thrown in the air.

The fourth group was assigned to various tasks in the kitchen and courtyard. The Germans carefully inspected each pit, and the ashes, to ensure everything was destroyed. Special walls of white sheeting were erected to block any view of the operation but it was impossible to conceal the stench of burning bodies.

Captain Kolia Vassilenko, a Soviet prisoner-of-war, was brought to Fort IX and was put to work destroying evidence with the other prisoners. He immediately started planning an escape with them.

He studied the layout of Fort IX as well as the daily routine and housing of the guards. He revealed his plan of escape to only a few of the other working prisoners, waiting for the escape to near before sharing it with any more of the workers. Their first attempt at escape was to dig a tunnel out into the woods, it failed when their tunnel hit rock and they could go no further. After all the digging, and secretly hiding the dirt, they were forced to cease their work.

They thought about bribing the guards, but the guards already had all they wanted from the desecrated corpses. After several ideas were discarded, they finally agreed on a daring escape plan. Every night the prisoners were locked up in an underground cell with an overhead storeroom. They would make a key to the storeroom, which had a door leading to a tunnel in the courtyard of the Fort. From this tunnel, they would dig another tunnel to the outer wall of the Fort, but a thick steel door barred the tunnel from the storeroom. They had to find a way to open the steel door, without any tools.

Some of the prisoners worked in the Fort's workshops and were able to make a key that would open the door. Each day, two men would claim to be too sick to work and with a penknife found in the clothes of a rotting corpse and a drill they had stolen from a workshop, one of the men drilled through the steel door while the other kept watch.

It took weeks to drill holes and saw through the steel between the holes. They used a pile of rags to hide their progress. Keys were made to all underground cells and a collapsible wooden ladder was constructed. Wooden beams in the tunnels, that would have otherwise blocked their escape, had to be removed. The prisoners cleverly complained to the Germans that the wood used for the pyre was too wet to burn and requested that they use the wood from the tunnels. Permission was granted and it was plain sailing from there.

The date was set for the escape: December 25, 1943. They rehearsed the escape over and over. The tension was unbearable. They worried over every step and feared they would be replaced by other workers before their escape date. A commander was assigned to each of the four groups of escapees and each one was given explicit instructions. Finally, the appointed date arrived. The cigarettes and schnapps, in honor of Christmas, given to them by the Germans, were given to the guards to make them even more drunk.

Sometime after 8 p.m., the escape was set in motion. They opened all their cells, covered everything with blankets to deaden the sound, went through the steel door, and entered the tunnel. When they reached the outer wall of the fort, they put up screens of white sheets to obscure the view of the ladders being lowered to the ground. Finally, all 64 prisoners had reached their freedom!

Many of them went north to join the partisans in the woods, others moved west to set up their own partisan group, another group, which included the four women and a doctor went to the neighboring villages and the remaining 13, led by Captain Vassilenko, went to the Kovno Ghetto.

Those who went to the ghetto knocked on the doors of Underground leaders who concealed them in hiding places. The Germans began to terrorize people in their search for the escapees. Only 28 of the 64 escapees managed to find shelter and survive. The others were murdered by the Germans or Lithuanian collaborators. Tory, Chaim Yellen, the leader of the partisans, and Captain Vassilenko held a secret meeting. Vassilenko, speaking in Yiddish, told them about the escape plans and what he had seen happening at Fort IX. He had evidence and materials taken from the graves.

Eleven of the escapees wrote a memorandum, in Russian, on the day after arriving in the ghetto. They wrote about the work of the 64 prisoners assigned to destroy the corpses. They made two copies of this memorandum and stored one copy in the Underground archive, located in the ghetto, and the other was sent to the headquarters of the partisan units in Rudninkai. The partisans sent it to Moscow where it was read out, live, on Radio Moscow.

VIII. THE POLICE, OLD PEOPLE, AND CHILDREN'S AKTIONS. MARCH 27-28, 1944

"That there is in this world neither brains, nor goodness, nor good sense, but only brute force. Bloodshed. Starvation. Death. That there was not the slightest hope even a glimmer of hope, of justice being done. It would never happen. No one would ever do it. The world was just one big Babi Yar. And there two great forces had come against each other and were striking against each other like hammer and anvil, and the wretched people were in between, with no way out; each individual wanted only to live and not be maltreated, to have something to eat, and yet they howled and screamed and in their fear they were grabbing at each other's throats, while I, little blob of watery jelly, was sitting in the midst of this dark world. Why? What for? Who had done it all? There was nothing, after all to hope for! Winter. Night." A. Anatoli Kuznetsov

The Jewish police force was divided into three precincts, each with its own captain. Publicly they carried out orders from the Germans but in secret they worked with the Underground.

The ghetto gates were patrolled by the Jewish police and lazy German soldiers who didn't take note of much. The Jewish police would let the Underground members smuggle weapons into a secret warehouse where they trained young people and stored contraband. They also let people who had joined the Underground leave and help smuggle children out of the ghetto. Eventually, the Germans became suspicious and many of the Jewish police force were executed.

A few days after the Aktion in October 1941, Captain Jordan brought 1,000 Rubles to the Council for distribution among the airport workers and informed the Council that Jewish workers were required to work every shift at the airport. Captain Jordan said that the fate of the Jews depended on the Council's ability to provide airport workers.

Registration of all the Jews was carried out by the labor office. At first, they demanded 500 men every evening, but it was soon increased to 1,000. It was impossible to get enough men, the police had to drag people to the collection point at the gate. They would gather at four o'clock in the afternoon and leave for the airfield at six o'clock in the evening and return at seven o'clock the next morning. The men weren't given anything to eat while they waited or worked.

The work was back-breaking. They had to dig dirt, mix and carry cement. At first, the Wehrmacht soldiers guarding them didn't treat them badly but eventually they started to strike and beat the workers. The trucks that transported the Jews to and from the airport were discarded and in addition to standing on their feet without food, for 15 hours, they had to walk the 16 kilometers between the airfield and the ghetto.

On November 8, 1941, we were ordered to appear before the Labor Committee in a large square that was lit entirely by big searchlights. We were assembled into rows of 100 and, accompanied by the Jewish police, were sent to the gate to be transported to the airport. This happened every day so it became a routine. As time went on, people would slack off from this daily obligation and it became the job of the Jewish police to go from house to house and route out the stragglers.

We worked in two shifts. The airport day shift that left at 2 p.m. kept the police occupied, filling the quota for this shift until all the rows finished departing at 4 p.m. The police then had to go back to the ghetto and begin gathering workers for the night shift. The police had to enter houses, crawl over and under beds, check attics, check documents, and any other possible hiding places. Eventually, the Germans reduced the two shifts to one shift, but the grueling and strenuous work continued for six months.

The Germans then created task forces of skilled workers. These people were treated decently by the Germans and had the opportunity to bring food home to their families. The airport workers resented them and would refuse to report to work.

Once, not enough workers reported for work at the gate so the Germans shot six people. This made it clear that work schedules were needed to ensure that everyone took turns working at the airport. At first, the ghetto police took turns working at the airport too, but it became apparent that they were needed to help round up people in the ghetto.

On March 27, 1944, Jews who had jobs were sent to them; some to the airfield, some to the workshops, and some to the city and the ghetto. The only people left at home were children, the sick, and the elderly. At about 8.30 a.m., an Aktion began with the appearance of additional guards around the ghetto fence.

The Jewish police were meeting in the commander's yard, awaiting new orders. Quite suddenly, buses with painted windows pulled up and the Jewish policemen were ordered to crawl on all fours into the buses. The policemen realized that they were being taken to Fort IX. Those who attempted to escape were shot immediately. At Fort IX, the men were stripped of all their belongings and cruelly beaten. They were tortured in an attempt to get information about hidden cellars and resistance workers. Because the Jewish police knew little about the resistance and their operations, no incriminating information was revealed to the Germans. Nevertheless, the Jewish chief of police and his immediate assistants, a total of 40, were shot and killed.

Bullhorns announced that all ghetto residents were to stay in their homes and anybody found in the street would be shot. The Gestapo went from house to house and threw the elderly and children onto the street. Aunt Rosa was made to take her child outside to be collected. They dragged the child away from my aunt, put the child into a truck, and then set it on fire. My aunt, after witnessing this, went mad. I cannot talk about it to this day.

The German beasts went to each house and collected screaming children. People gave their children sedatives and hid them under mattresses or bundles of clothes. When frantic mothers ran after their children, they were beaten and stabbed with bayonets. Huge dogs attacked them and ripped at their flesh. Loudspeakers were blasting music to mute the desperate screams. On that day, 1,000 young lives were taken or snuffed out in the gas chambers of Auschwitz.

The Nazis knew, from their meticulously kept records, the number of children still in the ghetto and they also knew exactly how many had already been taken. They worked out that there were still more children, hiding.

The next day, buses filled with SS men and Lithuanians drove into the ghetto. They brought bloodhounds, axes, and picks along with them. There was complete panic throughout the ghetto as the Germans cracked walls, smashed floors, and threw hand grenades in their search for the hiding children. Another 800 children were found and were later murdered at Fort IX.

I was home that day, as was my brother-in-law, Misha, and my mother-in-law. When we heard the announcement, we weren't sure what to do. I looked at my brother-in-law, and he looked at me, and I said that we should hide my mother-in-law somewhere. Before we had a chance to do anything, the guards broke into the room and told her to get out of the bed. My mother-in-law, an exceptionally wonderful woman who was a pharmacist by profession, a fabulous cook and taught me how to make gourmet dishes, was a semi-invalid and couldn't walk. I stood in front of her and said that she couldn't walk. They slapped me and shouted, "She can't walk? So, you carry her!" I asked Misha to dress her properly as she was only wearing a nightgown. But they wouldn't even let us do that. Misha grabbed her by her shoulders and I had to grab her by the feet. I pulled her dress down – it would've broken my husband's heart to see her with her nightgown pulled up.

We carried her out to the street, a nightmarish scene that I will never forget. All you could see were young people carrying old people like animals, screaming. We carried her to where the buses were located, and a German, so young that the milk was still on his lips, told Misha to stay and told me to carry her on to the bus. She was a frail woman, so I was able to pick her up and get on the bus. There were no seats available, so I had to put her in the aisle and cover her up. I looked around to find a seat for myself but there were none. I thought they would kill me but they pushed me down the steps and said that I had to get out. That was the last time we saw her. They killed her. The Germans were determined to rid the ghetto of all the unproductive and weak.

My mother had a stroke after her brother, Rachmeal, was killed in an Aktion and she had a severe limp. I knew she would be in trouble and ran over to her apartment to see what I could do to save her. I found my brother there, applying lots of makeup to my mother's face to make her look younger, which was just like my wonderful brother. He had left work to take care of her when he heard about the Aktion. He told her to stay seated so the Germans wouldn't see her limp. When the Germans arrived, they looked at her but left her alone.

We all felt so trapped, but there was nothing we could do and there was no one willing to help us. Rumors circulated that the Russians were going to invade soon. All we could do was to hope that this was true and that the Russians would indeed arrive soon.

While this was happening, three people from the ghetto were sent on a special mission to break into the house of one of the murdered policemen, remove two tin boxes and bury them in holes they had dug. In 1964, 20 years later, the boxes were accidentally discovered, and appeared to contain a ghetto archive of 30,000 pages. Within the pages, life in the ghetto was described and the concerts given by the Jewish police orchestra were explained. This orchestra performed many concerts and was even attended, and enjoyed, by the SS. When the police were arrested, the members of the orchestra weren't killed, instead, they were sent to Dachau where they continued to play. Many survived the war and played in the refugee camps.

IX. THE JOURNEY BEGINS

"That they were torn from mistakes they had no chance to fix;
everything unfinished. All the sins of love without detail, detail
without love. The regret of having spoken, of having run out of
time to speak. Of hoarding oneself. Of turning one's back too
often in favor of sleep. I tried to imagine their physical needs, the
indignity of human needs grown so extreme they equal your
longing for wife, child, sister, parent, friend. But truthfully, I
couldn't even begin to imagine the trauma of their hearts, of being
taken in the middle of their lives. Those with young children. Or
those newly in love, wrenched from that state of grace. Or those
who had lived invisibly, who were never known."
Anne Michaels

Despite the lack of radios and phones, communication within the ghetto thrived. It was 1944 and somehow, we knew that the ghetto was to be destroyed the next day. We also knew that the Russians were closing in and the Germans were on the run. Before they left, the Germans had orders to destroy the ghetto. My husband and I just had to survive a few more days.

People built sophisticated underground bunkers, or *malinas*, where they hid until the Russians arrived. We asked for space in many of them but were told they were filled to capacity. We decided to dig our own malinas but it was more of a hole in the ground. As it turned out, more than 1,000 Jews hid in malinas, all but one were destroyed by the Germans when they burned down the city.

We dug a large hole in the backyard and filled it with some crackers and a large bottle of water. Around midnight, we bunkered down into this muddy hideout. I found some straw and a green pillow in the house, resembling grass, that we could use to cover the hole. We waited for what seemed like hours before the Germans entered the yard, yelling that there must be people here because the door was open. Suddenly a boot pushed the pillow onto our heads and the Germans started screaming and pointed guns in the hole. All muddy, we were dragged out of the hole and made to stand against the wall.

The Germans thought there were more Jews in the hole and searched for them. Just as we were about to be shot, an Austrian officer yelled, "Stop, don't shoot them. Let's take them." He then looked at us and said, "Look how muddy you are. Look how dirty you are. Go clean yourselves up and we will take you to a much better place." He had saved us, only to send us to a concentration camp.

The Germans opened the door and told us to walk. The scene outside made it look like a parade, with hundreds of people walking in the direction of the trains. We had no choice but to walk out of the ghetto and into trains that would take us to Germany. Since we were permitted to take something with us, I took the coat in which my father had hidden the mink skins. We walked through the streets with heavy hearts and in total fear of what the future held. Eventually, we arrived at the train-cattle cars. They pushed us onto the train and packed us in like sardines. I could barely breathe. It was awful. It was sheer hell!

The Germans would transport people to different places to work. They mostly kept people on the waterfront because transportation on the Yemen River was abundant. My brother would often go to the river, take off his yellow Star of David, and blend in.

When the Germans were closing the ghetto and when he was in line with everybody else to get on a train, he removed the star and escaped. That was the last time I saw him. We searched for him everywhere after the war, in Israel, in all the displaced persons' camps and we put our names on every list we could but didn't find him. Perhaps, his so-called friends were bribed and turned him in but I believe that if he was alive, he would've found us.

Families desperately held onto one another so they wouldn't be separated. I found my mother and father, and Ralph found Misha and sister-in-law on the train. The first stop was Stutthof where the women were told to get off. The train then continued to Dachau, where the men were imprisoned. They told us we would meet up with our husbands and fathers later on. Ralph, my father, and Misha were sent to Dachau where my father died not long after their arrival.

The Germans' contempt for the Jews was so consuming that when leaving Kovno, making sure they eradicated every Jew, they burned the city to the ground. When the Soviet army liberated

Kovno on August 1, 1944, of the original 35,000 Jews in Kovno, only 500 Jews had survived in forests or in bunkers. An additional 2,500 were sent to concentration camps in Germany. When people ask me how I survived, I say I was lucky and that's all I can say – I was just lucky. There is no other answer. None.

George Kadish/Zvi Kadushin. *Destruction of Kovno Ghetto*. Circa August 1944 – October 1944. US Holocaust Memorial Museum Hidden History of the Kovno Ghetto.

Photographer unknown. *Surviving Jews gathered outside the burnt remnants of the Kovno ghetto*. 1944. Holocaust Education and Archive Research Team.

X. ARRIVAL AT STUTTHOF

"I shall never forget how I was roused one night by the groans of a fellow prisoner, who threw himself about in his sleep, obviously having a horrible nightmare. Since I had always been especially sorry for people who suffered from fearful dreams or deliria, I wanted to wake the poor man. Suddenly I drew back the hand which was ready to shake him, frightened at the thing I was about to do. At that moment I became intensely conscious of the fact that no dream, no matter how horrible, could be as bad as the reality of the camp which surrounded us, and to which I was about to recall him."
Viktor E. Frankl, *Man's Search for Meaning*

My mother, my sister-in-law and I got off the train and were piled into open trucks to be taken to Stutthof. They took us to a clearing where a few young soldiers were seated at what looked like picnic tables. I held onto my coat for dear life but they took it away with whatever else I had, which was very little. They told us to disrobe, and by that, they meant we needed to take everything off.

Hundreds of women, mothers, and daughters undressed, and stood completely naked in front of the young thugs.

I kept thinking that these people weren't human, they are creatures from another planet or sent here from Hell. I didn't bother worrying about them when they looked at me. How humiliated can you feel when you're standing with your mother, relatives, and friends? I kept silently repeating to myself that I was going to survive this. I told my mother that we would make it. We would make it because it's not real. How can it be real: a picnic table with three or four young men and all these naked women standing in front of them?

They took some women aside to examine if they had hidden jewelry in their private areas. They told us to go in through the back of a building to take showers and get our uniforms, the striped uniforms of the Stutthof concentration camp. Our suffering had only just begun.

They took us to a nice-looking place, containing barracks with bunk beds, like the ones you see in Holocaust Museums today. They brought us some soup which I shared with my mother because some of hers had spilled.

We were on the top tier of the bunk beds and below us were another mother and daughter. When the soup came we heard the daughter say to her mother, "You don't need that soup. Give it to me." I don't know how long I was there for, but it was awful, totally terrible. Mothers taking food from their children, daughters eating the food that belonged to their mothers. People were destroying each other. I think the Germans knew how people would react and had indeed planned it that way. I said to myself, "My God, what a world."

The next day they called us to gather in a large open area. There were just a few German boys taking care of us. They were all young and well-groomed. They started separating us. I was standing with my mother, as were other girls and their mothers.

My mother was only 39 years old, young, blond and beautiful. They grabbed her away from me and when I ran after her they hit me and ordered me to get into an open-roofed truck. That was the last time I saw my mother. After they took her away from me, I was left with my sister-in-law but I only wanted to follow my mother. My resistance to following orders only provoked rough treatment from the Germans.

We were in the truck and a girl came over and asked if she could be my friend. Having a friend meant someone would look out for you, and vice versa. While agreeing, I noticed she was tall and good-looking. That was Zlata, a very good-natured and loving person. Her mother and one of her sisters were taken away from her. We remained friends, even after the war, and I kept in touch with her as long as I could. I looked her up on Skype a few times and it worked until about a year ago. Unfortunately, she has Alzheimer's and doesn't know who I am anymore.

It was important to attach yourself to the right woman and everyone was watching to see who would share a spot with whom when they eventually placed us somewhere. There was room to move around on the truck, so there was a lot of talking. Another girl came over to where we were seated and asked if she could join us. Her name was Yochevet, older than me, and an exceptionally warm, giving, and wonderful woman. She had dark hair, dark eyes, and a perpetual smile. Just by looking at her, you could see that you could count on her to do anything for a friend. She was a truly wonderful person. I was in touch with her until she passed away in the 70s.

Another friend, Rachel or Ruchel, was about four or five years older, and was married. Her husband was a reporter for the *Yiddishe Shtimer* in Kovno. She had a child who was taken away from her and she also left a child with Lithuanians. She and her husband eventually made it to Manhattan and lived there for a while before moving to Haifa, Israel.

The Germans, always methodical, gave everyone registration numbers. These numbers determined the work camp and the groups for evacuation. My number was 42018 and Zlata's was 41410.[1]

In his book, *The Extermination of Jews in Stutthof Concentration Camp 1939-1945*, Danuta Drywa describes the establishment of filial camps. The book includes registers of names of Jews incarcerated in KL Stutthof in the years 1939 to 1942; of Jewish inmates transferred from KL Auschwitz to KL Stutthof on February 8, 1943; of Jews from the Riga ghetto, shot and drowned on the beach at Neustadt (current-day Wejherowo, Poland); and a table of transports of Jewish inmates, June 29 to October 28, 1944.

The Stutthof concentration camp was established in September 1939, with about 150 Polish citizens as the first inmates. Prisoners were often sick, and many died during typhus epidemics in 1942 and 1944.

The Germans began gassing inmates with Zyklon B in 1944 when Stuffhof was included in the 'Final Solution'. From 1939 to 1944, Jews were a minority in the camp, but in the latter part of 1944 they became the vast majority. The rapid growth of the inmate population in 1944 created a problem for assigning labor directly within the camp, so between 1942 and 1944, 32 smaller camps were established. In all, 26,251 Jews were employed, of which

23,649 were women. These prisoners, selected by age and ability to work, provided unskilled laborers at airfields, factories, or other industries.[2] It is difficult to determine which of the 32 camps I was sent to. Zlata seems to remember that we were assigned to a sub-camp at the airfield in Pruszcz Gdański/Praust.[3]

As the Russian offense intensified, the Germans began to liquidate the sub-camps. We were made to march under deplorable conditions. Some were beaten, stabbed with bayonets, starved, drowned, and shot as we walked. Many were killed by lethal injection or died of typhoid fever or typhus. These marches have been referred to as 'Death Marches' and my description of my Death March coincides with the description of prisoners from several sub-camps, all converging at Chynow (Chinow), liberated on March 10, 1945.

---

1. Zilber, Ettie, *A Holocaust Memoir of Love and Resilience*, Amsterdam Publishers, 2019, pp. 49, 50
2. Drywa, Danuta, *The Extermination of Jews in Stutthof Concentration Camp 1939-1945*, Stutthof Museum in Sztutowo, 2004, p. 173
3. Zilber, Ettie, *A Holocaust Memoir of Love and Resilience*, Amsterdam Publishers, 2019, p. 118

XI. THE SHOES THAT SAVED ME

"We are the shoes, we are the last witnesses.
We are shoes from grandchildren and grandfathers
From Prague, Paris and Amsterdam,
And because we are only made of fabric and leather
And not of blood and flesh,
Each one of us avoided the hellfire."
Moshe Szulsztein

The Germans placed us in tents, about 60 women in each, where, for a year, we lived and slept naked on straw-covered ground. The tents were very primitive and surrounded by wire. You could cross the wires and make a run for it, but the Germans weren't concerned about this, they knew there was nowhere for us to go. Every morning we would get up, eat breakfast – some hot water with vegetables, presumably – and then we went out to work. We dug deep ditches in the woods near a lake and I have no idea what they did with these ditches.

The labor was intense and the Germans were without mercy. They stood over us to make sure we didn't take any breaks; they would hit you if you stopped, even for a second. To avoid being hit, I made sure I never stopped working. I made myself believe that they weren't going to bring me down to their level. It was winter and so cold but even though it was freezing, we would break up the ice on the lake and get in the water to wash. The biggest demoralization was the filth. The filth, the stench, and the lice were indescribable.

My friends and I decided we were going to reduce the filth by hook or by crook. The women around us were filthy, especially the older ones. The young women just gave up, they didn't care, but we promised one another two things: we were going to keep our feet covered and our bodies clean. With the snow, winter came, and as soon as someone got sick, it was the end of them. The Germans, hoping to decrease the population, didn't tolerate sickness of any kind. If someone got sick, they were sent to the infirmary and they never came back.

When we returned from digging ditches, we would try, as much as possible, to keep ourselves clean. We used to take our clothes, whatever little we had, especially underwear, and try to rinse and dry them by placing them on a wood-burning stove, situated in the middle of the tent. Can you imagine 60 naked women gathered around a stove, all trying to dry their tattered clothes? One woman, who was most unpleasant and rude, a terror, and she always had more than anyone else. She, self-appointed, was in charge of the stove and would fight with everyone. I would run away whenever I saw her, I didn't want to start anything with her. We had never even had a conversation.

Winters were cold, but I was lucky enough to have good shoes. Every so often, perhaps twice a year, the Germans would come with a truck containing shoes and warm clothes. They used to throw them at us and whoever caught something was lucky.

I managed to catch a nice pair of shoes that covered my toes, but my sister-in-law, who was with me, along with three other women, got shoes that were a size too small, so they suffered constantly. There were five of us who always stuck together. We took care of each other, supported each other, and shared our food with one another. We all followed the rules. I figured that if I had to stand on my head, naked, to stay alive, I would. When we were in Stutthoff there were rumors that the Germans were going to sterilize us. It never happened but during our time there, we didn't get our periods.

In *A Holocaust Memoir of Love & Resilience* Zlata recalls,

"Friendship was extremely important. I was all alone in the camp. One day when we were lined up for roll call, I found myself standing next to four other girls/women because our registration numbers were similar. It was Henny, Tanya, Rochel, Yocheved and me. Three were much older and were nurses, Henny was my age. We decided to stay together. We shared everything and took care of each other. We shared food and we slept in the same bunk. We even shared the brown water – supposedly coffee – so we could wash our hair. We were afraid of getting lice. Another important factor for survival was a sense of humor, Henny had the best sense of humor. We had wooden bunks where we slept together on straw. We slept close together to stay warm and would joke at night about the things we dreamed about for the future... "[1]

The war was ending and the Germans were losing, but they wouldn't give up. Their first priority was to kill the Jews. They began moving us from one town to another. They received continuous orders as to which camp or area to occupy so as to get rid of us as quickly as possible. We used to stop to sleep, usually in a large barn, every night. Sometimes they would give us some food, although not often enough.

We kept losing people along the way, especially those who didn't have shoes, they died of hypothermia and frostbitten feet. Luckily, I had a good pair of shoes.

Women died along the road. People sometimes asked how I felt about seeing people die. It's incredible that when you live amidst the dying and death, you get accustomed to it. Death was an everyday occurrence and I didn't think about it or anything else. It's unbelievable, unthinkable, that people so young could be so cruel.

The Germans who were marching and killing us couldn't have been older than 20. When I saw someone lying in the snow, being shot, it became something normal. It's terrible to admit, but that's how I felt. You don't look, you just walk. The Germans used to shoot women as soon as they saw them struggling or sitting down. That's why, when I lost my shoes, I knew I wasn't going to make it far before dying.

I was so cold and hungry, but my determination to survive outweighed my suffering. When people are dying or being killed, the initial shock is terrible, but then you do get used to it. The only thing pushing you forward is the thought of making it out alive. If you had to ask me what stood out the most during that walk – death stood out, only death.

Every night, we would ask the Germans how long we'd be staying at the barn for. Sometimes it would be for a while, so I, being the brave one, would go to a neighboring village and knock on doors to ask for bread.

They knew who we were, Jews, and not worth anything. But they gave me bread before telling me to leave. They were terrified that they would get caught giving me food, but they were always willing to help, and I never had any problems getting food. These people would have to be blind not to see what was happening. Perhaps, because they knew the war was coming to an end, they wanted to do something for us. I would eat as much of the food as I possibly could and then take the rest back to my friends.

We arrived at a barn one night, near Chynow. This barn would eventually be our last stop and the place we would be killed. The Germans told us we were going to stay there until noon the next day and then we would begin our walk again. My sister-in-law asked if she could borrow my shoes, there was snow on the ground and she wanted to go into the village and get us bread. She hadn't done this before and wanted the chance to contribute so I gave her my shoes thinking she would come back with them and bread.

She never came back and by noon, the Germans told us to start walking again. I later found out that she had knocked on a door and asked the occupant to hide her there. She had escaped with my shoes and left me with hers that I couldn't wear as they were much too small for me. I knew I was going to die, just like all the others had, on the road. I told myself that I wouldn't give the Germans the satisfaction of seeing me die on the street, like a dog. My friends said they would carry me, but I refused. There was no way I could leave the barn, knowing what awaited me.

Then a woman, the one who was a terror, who had fought with everybody, came over to me and handed me a pair of shoes that she had tied over her shoulder. The first and only words she would ever say to me were, "Here, I have an extra pair of shoes for you." I could never explain why she did this and I never saw her again. I don't even know her name, but she saved my life with a pair of shoes. I looked for her after the war for many years, but never found her.

Years later, after my sister-in-law left me to die, the first thing she said to me was, "I came back, but you were gone." She was quite different from me, helpless, and attached herself to me like a child. I never forgave her, but I don't hate her, when you hate people you eventually hate yourself.

The last time I saw her was in Israel and she had a very bad case of Alzheimer's. She was sitting in a chair and was fed by someone else. When I came in, she stopped eating and just stared at me. Her husband and children knew what she had done to me and I didn't keep it a secret. Her kids knew how selfishly she had acted, even under those conditions. She found an opportunity to escape and disregarded everything and everyone else. She knew that I would die without my shoes, we had both seen the women without shoes freezing to death. She had shoes, but they were a little too small and she didn't want to be uncomfortable. She didn't care.

You're probably asking why they made us march instead of simply killing us. For the answer, you would have to understand the Germans' thinking. This was partly accomplished by the examination of recorded interrogations of captured German prisoners of war and soldiers.

In their book *Soldaten*, Sonke Neitzel and Harald Welzer studied these interrogations. Harald Welzer, a social psychologist and Sonkde Neitzel, a historian, discovered thousands of pages of reported interrogations in the British National Archives and the National Archives in Washington, D.C. Combining their disciplines, they were able to examine the frames of reference from which the soldiers operated in order to explain their behavior.

They were able to digitize most of the material and sort through it with the assistance of content recognition software. After three years of sorting through this tremendous amount of material, they were able to present their work in *Soldaten*.

They theorize that German soldiers were aware of the Holocaust but the number of discussions about the subject was limited compared to discussions about military techniques and conquests. The extermination of Jews was spoken about but was not as important to them as other war topics. Conversations about the mass murdering of Jews centralized more on the methods utilized, how to improve the procedure of elimination, and how to kill as many as possible in the most expedient fashion, rather than on the act itself. The soldiers believed that the murders were destiny and didn't consider them to be unjust – it was just something that needed to happen.

Many conversations between soldiers were recorded and presented in this book. Reports include descriptions by soldiers on how they participated in mass murders, either by invitation or voluntarily. There are descriptions of how local residents showed up to watch the spectacle of Jews being murdered and demonstrated that these actions were by no means secret, and contrary to their denials, many knew exactly what was happening. Even bans on watching these murders were ignored. Execution tourism, as it was called, was the killing of Jews on an open-air stage as civilians, among them women and children, looked on.

One soldier reported, "The SS issued an invitation to go and shoot Jews. All the troops went along with rifles and… shot them up.

Each man could pick the one he wanted. [...] It was sent out like an invitation to a hunt."[2]

The Germans were extremely obedient – like well-trained dogs. German children, *Hitlerjuge*nd, as young as eight years old were taught that Jews weren't human, to never look them in the eye, that Jews were a menace to society and they were encouraged to kill Jews too. Because of their obedience, they did as they were told, regardless of morality.

The Germans wanted us to suffer and history has shown that Germans were bred to hate and poison minds. They were dangerous people, starting two world wars without thought, only obedience.

---

1. Zilber, Ettie, *A Holocaust Memoir of Love and Resilience*, Amsterdam Publishers, 2019, p. 92, Zlata's recollection of meeting Henny is different to Henny's recollection.
2. Neitzel, Sönke & Welzer, Harald, *Soldaten: On Fighting, Killing, and Dying*, Simon & Schuster UK Ltd, 2012, p. 211

XII. CHYNOW

"Meanwhile the dead were fallen all about me,
Nor were they interred by usual rites:
Too many funeral crowded temple gates...
And none were left
To weep their loss: unwept the souls of matrons,
Of brides, young men and ancients – all vanished
To the blind wilderness of wind..."
Anne Michaels

Eventually, we circled back to Chynow, the last village of the death march. By then, the Germans knew they had lost the war and that the Russians were closing in. We were put in a huge barn – it was like Dante's Inferno because everybody was dying. I wouldn't be surprised if 85 percent of the people in the barn died there. Diarrhea, the stench, and the frozen corpses made it a living hell. Every place you sat was next to a corpse.

There were women from all over gathered there, not only from our tent near Stutthof. Women from tents, near where we dug ditches, joined us in the barn. There were probably about 500 women in the barn. We knew they were going to murder us there.

We spent several days among the dead and dying. There were women scattered everywhere, lying on scraps of straw, some of them quite obviously with the mark of death on their faces. Half of them were already dead. We were sleeping with corpses. Nothing could compare to this, being treated as less than human. We were innocent, but not in the eyes of the Germans.

We buried the dead when we could, carrying them out to big ditches the Germans had made us dig when we first arrived. My friend who sat next to me in school, came over to me, seeing that I was still able to walk, and asked if I would help bury her mother. With her assistance, I carried her mother out to the mass grave and dropped her on a pile of bones.

I went back to the barn and, with the exception of my friends, was surrounded by death once again. Of the five of us who had stuck together, one had escaped on the way and another escaped with my shoes. Three of us remained and held on to each other when we could. We were relatively healthy, so we helped with burying people. We would dig the holes and another group would bring the corpses. A rumor spread that the Germans were going to pour gasoline around the barn and set it on fire, with us inside. That would be the end of the life we had lived if you can call it a life.

The barn was set up like an amphitheater, but instead of concrete there was only straw. The rows were stacked closely together and those behind us had their feet on our shoulders. We sat in the first row, right next to the barn doors.

On March 10, 1945, after being in the barn for about three or four days, we heard voices and barn door closing. The Germans poured gasoline all around the barn and their intention became clear: they were going to burn the whole barn. We knew that was the end, that the horror would be over and there was no way out.

We waited, and ten minutes later, somebody started banging, very hard, on the barn doors. We heard: "*Me Ruskie* (I am Russian), we are here to help you." The hatred the Germans had for us was unfathomable. They were no more than 20 years old and they knew the Russians were only minutes away. Yet, they had already spread gasoline around half of the barn in order to burn us alive. As soon as the doors opened, and because we were seated right next to them, the three of us ran out. I was the first one out because I could walk. One of my friends, too weak, had to be dragged out.

A Russian got hold of me, handed me a rifle and told me to shoot the Germans. The Russians were ready to kill them and they wanted us to help. There were only five or six young Germans guarding the barn. The rest had run away. Even though my heart was filled with hatred for them, I dropped the gun. I wasn't going to pull the trigger and act like the Germans.

Years ago, I was invited to a cocktail party hosted by an organization that supports education about the Holocaust. I was the only survivor present. A man approached me asked, "How come so many Jews weren't able to retaliate against those people who were killing you? They were so young. How did you let them do it?"

I looked at him and said, "Think of yourself being surrounded by vicious dogs and if you had a chance to break away from them and escape, you would eventually encounter another set of vicious dogs. We were surrounded. Nobody was going to help us even if we could escape. My brother, who had so many Lithuanian friends, who didn't look Jewish, took his star off when they were loading us on the train. He walked away, probably thinking his friends would help him, but nobody did. He never made it. You cannot visualize what happened. It's impossible. There was nowhere to go. If you could escape, and if people were friendly, then maybe you stood a chance. But that was not the case".

XIII. THE HOUSE

"To share a hiding place,
physical or psychological,
is as intimate as love."
Anne Michaels

We ran all the way to Chynow, a little village in German-occupied Poland, and found it completely deserted with doors and homes left open. We could pick any of the houses in which to hide, but we wanted to get as far away from that barn as possible. We finally chose a house, locked the doors, and rejoiced in our new-found freedom. We could think of nothing else but food. Thrilled and terrified we started to search, and to our amazement, we found jars and jars full of food. The Germans had a way of preserving food in glass jars and the cabinets were loaded with them.

During our hunt for food, we noticed a cow through the window. One of my friends suggested that we milk the cow and when I volunteered for the job, no one objected; they knew I was the most daring of the group. I had never milked a cow before and figured that I would do what I had seen done in the movies. I started pulling and pulling at the cow's udders, filling the container with milk. But I don't think I was doing it correctly, or maybe, the cow just didn't like me. In one swift movement, the cow kicked out its hind leg and knocked the bucket, filled with milk, over. We were fortunate that the milk spilled, because we hadn't eaten in so long, too much milk in our bodies may have killed us.

The cabinets were full of meats and other food items, but we restrained from eating it all at once, as to not overwhelm our bodies. We locked ourselves in and stayed there for about two weeks. Two of my friends came down with typhoid fever and I had to take care of them. We hoped that somebody would eventually save us. Russians came once, and banged on the door, yelling, "Let us in, we want to sleep, we want to rest." We refused to open the door, knowing that they would rape us, even if we were sick. Somehow, we always knew when we were in danger. It became our sixth sense. You always know, when your life depends on it.

One evening, a man knocked on the door and said, first in Russian, "Let me in, I am a Jew." Then he said, *"Ich red Yiddish. Kub in nish shloffen in feir tug. Luz meer legen in your potogin.* I won't touch anybody." I told him we were sick and there was no place for him to sleep. But he kept saying in Yiddish that he was exhausted and had to sleep. We looked at one another and everybody grabbed something to defend themselves with – a frying pan, a broom – we opened the door and said it was okay for him to come in. He was a Russian Jewish soldier, a nice guy.

We had to find a place for him to sleep for the night. I was sleeping in one bed with one of my friends and the other women were in the other bed. We told him to sleep on the floor and created a make-shift bed for him. In the middle of the night, however, my friend and I awoke to discover the man had crawled into bed between us, with his rifle, to sleep. Too scared, we didn't sleep for the rest of the night. He got up in the morning and left. Then the typhoid got me and my friends helped me recover.

One day, to my amazement, my Aunt Lena came to see us. That she had found us is an example of how efficient the Underground communication was. She gave us a basket of food and left. I never saw her again after our meeting in Paris – I heard she had her leg amputated and died. It's difficult to visualize it. Here you were surrounded by horrible people, killing and performing heinous acts, but other people seemed to live a normal life. My being alive and telling my story is all down to luck. I never thought I would make it.

We were under Russian care and they knew the houses were occupied by the Jews who had been saved from the large barn. They visited each house to tell us when we would be taken back to Lithuania. Even though we were cut off from the rest of the world, we managed to get up-to-date information.

Jewish agencies were placed in various areas and would always have information, especially pertaining to the whereabouts of loved ones, available. It's unbelievable how people found one another after the war, my husband managed to find me in Lodz, without a train timetable or telephones. We relied heavily on mouth-to-mouth communication for train schedules as the trains seemed to go wherever they wanted to. You had no way of knowing the destination or direction of the train journey. We only knew that the trains didn't go west, which was into Europe.

XIV. THE ROAD TO FREEDOM

The Russians told us that we would be going east and, eventually, they would take us back to Lithuania. They told us that we first had to go to a central meeting point. We were concerned, we had heard that the Russians were sending people to places other than where they came from. Because so many of us were sick and needed hospitalization or immediate medical assistance, getting us to gather together was impossible.

We were finally taken east, by bus, to Gdansk (Danzig). We stopped in various towns along the way to eat and rest, the Russians fed us water and potatoes. Older women told us to hide at night, fearful of the Russians and their tendency to take advantage of women. One night, resting in a school, we were told to hide under the desks.

We finally reached Gdansk, a Russian enclave in Poland. We were given a large apartment, on the third floor of a five-story building, to live in. The ground floor was occupied by the Russian military in charge of us and we surmised that we were going to be taken to

Russia, not Lithuania. We would have to figure out a way to escape.

My friend, Rachel, asked me to escape with her and to leave my other friends behind. I told her I wouldn't leave the other girls, I'll never forget her disloyalty. Zlata saw me talking to her and asked me about the conversation. When I told her that Rachel wanted me to escape with her, Zlata started crying.

Rachel did a terrible thing – asking me to leave the others. She wanted me to leave Yocheved, a gentle soul, who, unfortunately, married a very religious man in Israel and later lived in a religious community. Yocheved was a wonderful nurse who worked in the Jewish hospital in Lithuania before the war, a real *goldena nashama*. Rachel wanted me to leave Zlata, who was my best friend and a wonderful person.

Rachel had left her child in a convent for the duration of the war. She was older than us and was married to a man who worked for the newspaper in Kovno. His name was Gar. During the war, people knew the Germans were also killing all Jewish babies they could find and I think, Rachel must have made some connections in Lithuania during the Russian occupation, because her connection, probably a nun, told her she could leave her child at a convent. Many people did that. She gave her child away not knowing if she would ever see him again.

She never found out what happened to the child and she wound up in Israel where her husband worked for a newspaper in Tel Aviv.

Rachel talked Yocheved into leaving with her. Zlata and I remained and the Russians paired us with two other women, who were planning to go to South Africa (see picture). The Russians gave each of us jobs to fill the time.

Zlata was sent to a farm to work during the day, the two other women were sent to load and unload things near the river, and I was sent to guard horses. They were kept in a large barn on the property, next to the building that housed us. These were special horses, not race horses, raised by the government.

They gave me a gun and showed me how to fire it. I suppose they chose me for this job because I looked tough. They told me not to let anyone get close to me and to make sure nothing happened to the horses. I was the night watchman and I stayed in a security booth in front of the compound. In the mornings, the Russians would pick me up from the booth and then take me back at night.

When people came to water the horses, I would check them in. Every morning, at around 6 a.m., a man would come and distribute fresh bread to the soldiers. On one particular morning, he spoke to me through the little window of my booth and told me that he wanted to give me something. He asked me to let him in, and because I saw him every day, I trusted him. Just as I was opening the door, he rushed in, straight at me. Knowing exactly what he was after, I grabbed the night light near me and threw it at him. He ran away.

Somehow, all through the war and after, I managed to hold onto my watch but after the altercation in the booth, it was broken. When I got back to the apartment, I told Zlata what happened, that the man had broken my watch and that I was going to go downstairs to report the incident to the soldiers. Zlata then said, "You're crazy. What are you going to report? You're a guard and you're not supposed to let anybody in. They'll send you away. Just stay where you are!" I listened to my good friend.

Zlata came home from work one day and told me that the owner of the farm wanted to marry her. Because we didn't know if anyone had been left alive, she thought it would be a wonderful idea. I looked at her and told her that she was crazy, that there was nothing on that farm for her, and to not leave me. Fortunately, she heeded my advice.

For most of the young women, this was not the case. They married anybody who they thought would take care of them. It was a horrible position to be in and I tried not to think about it. During the next couple of months, I decided that I would move to Israel, I knew the language and many of my school friends had relocated there. In school I had a good reputation and people looked up to me, so I knew I would have no trouble establishing a life there and I planned on going to a *Kibbutz*.

Zlata's father-in-law, amazingly, found us, Zlata was so excited she became hysterical. It was so chaotic after the war, people were seeking their families and loved ones through the Underground and the communication network was remarkable, no matter your location, there were always people who knew where to look for other people. If you got on a train, you would meet another Jew – somebody else who survived, and they would give you the news.

Zlata's father-in-law had found her and now wanted to take her with him. He was very fond of her and she believed he was a wonderful man. He was young, healthy, handsome, and charming. He had survived the war by hiding himself and his priority after the war was to find her, which he did. She worried about me because she couldn't take me with her. I told her that I would manage and that she had to go with him. He was going to Lodz, where there was an organization that acted as a clearinghouse. People went there searching for other people by registering their names and the people they were searching for.

Zlata's ghetto and Stutthoff experiences were eventually memorialized in a book written by her daughter, Ettie Zilber. *A Holocaust Memoir of Love and Resilience*, describes Zlata's life and Ettie's journey to the places where her mother was sent.

With Zlata gone, I decided to run away from the Russians. On Sundays, we were allowed to go see a movie. So, one Sunday, while everyone was at the movie, I packed my things, which wasn't much, into a little bundle, went out to the balcony and threw the bundle over and it landed not far from the gate that led out of the compound. I went down to the gate and picked up my belongings. I was terrified, perhaps even more than I had been of the Germans. I had no food or money but you didn't think about these things when the Germans were in charge because nobody had anything. Now I had nothing and left nothing behind.

At the gate, the guards asked me where I was going, I told them I was going to the movies and when they questioned the contents of my bundle, I told them, in Russian, that it was a pillow for the chair in the movie. When they told me I could go, I walked out and then started running, since I was sure they were after me with a brigade to look for me. It was terrifying. I didn't know the location of the train, but I knew that I would get there. I found the train and got in, even though I didn't know exactly where it was going. I knew it was going East, and that was enough.

I was looking around, trying to find somewhere to sit, and saw two young men in a compartment. They seemed harmless, they were sitting by themselves and because I was sure the Russians were on their way to stop the train and detain me, I sat down with them. We started talking, they asked me where I was from and I ended up telling them everything about myself. They turned out to be Jewish and from a very active Polish Underground whose members were mainly Jewish.

I asked them where they were going. They looked like students and were well dressed, and they told me they were going back to Lodz. The Underground there was helping people cross the borders. I thought very highly of them for their good deeds. They talked about the community in Lodz that helped locate people, as I had heard from Zlata's father-in-law. They invited me to relax, gave me cookies and candy from their abundant food stash, and said they would take me to Lodz. They assured me that everything would be fine.

We spent the rest of the train journey sleeping and talking. We disembarked the next morning, at 6 a.m., to miserable weather. They offered to buy me breakfast. I remember I wanted a donut filled with jelly, called a *ponchet* in Russian, so I asked them to get me something to drink and a ponchet. After breakfast, I decided that I would take a bus to Lodz. When I told them this, they looked at each other and then said, "Listen, there is a beautiful place here. We'll go and rent a room and we'll sleep for a little bit and then we'll take you tomorrow morning." I told them that was fine and to go ahead and rent the room.

As soon as they were out of sight I ran, as fast as I could, in the other direction. Thank goodness they were stupid enough to leave me behind, although I don't think they would have forced me to go with them since we were still so close to the train. In their minds, it must have seemed like I wanted to have a bit of fun with them.

I hopped into the first public bus I saw, and asked the driver – I spoke fluent Polish – for the location of where the refugees go to register.

Photographer unknown. *Henny & Friends*. 1945.
Courtesy of Steve Aronson. Photo taken two months
after the liberation on Gdansk. Second from left is Zlata,
Zlata's father-in-law, Henny, Yocheved.

Henny (on left) and Zlata in Miami. 2008. Steve Aronson.

XV. THE REUNION

"The giant jig-saw puzzle had over 6 million pieces, most of which tumbled down, carrying with them the tortured souls of millions. They fell to earth and were buried in crevices filled with the ashes of those before them. Ashes that fertilized the minds of those who created the puzzle. But how does one fit together the errant pieces, the ones that managed to escape the fall and were so misshapen that they no longer resembled their original shape? And when some fit together, how do they brush off the ashes of their past and find the glue to bind them?"
The author

I found the building where the committee was operating and I asked if anyone had inquired about me, they hadn't, but would tell me as soon as someone did. They told me to go upstairs if I needed somewhere to sleep. They were housed in an abandoned school and upstairs there was a very large room, that perhaps had been a gymnasium or cafeteria, with lots of mattresses and women on the floor. I found myself a corner mattress and went to sleep.

The next morning, I went downstairs and volunteered to work. I spoke Hebrew very well and helped out wherever I was needed. People started asking me where I wanted to go, I certainly was not planning on returning to Lithuania and I had always wanted to go to Israel. I signed up to go to Israel on the Exodus. I knew I would be comfortable in Israel.

In 1937, many of my classmates graduated and then moved to Israel or South Africa. Some of my friends made Aliyah in 1938 and lived in kibbutzim, so I knew I would be welcomed. Because I had no relatives that could help me out, I believed Israel was the place for me.

Mercifully, because the Germans had shaved our heads, we didn't need to worry about washing our hair. The other small blessing was that I didn't have my period for two or three years. Perhaps they injected us to stop our periods but I had no recollection of that being done. I think that the immense amount of stress we were under had changed our bodies. I had a turban and used it to cover my shaved head, just as the other women did. When I got up in the morning, I would put on my turban and go to the organization to inquire whether they had any jobs for me.

As I was going downstairs one day, I realized that I had forgotten to put my turban on. I went back to the room to collect it and then into the bathroom to put it on. When I walked out of the bathroom, a man was standing there, whom I instantly recognized as my husband, Raphael. His journey back to me was unbelievable and I was absolutely stunned. My prince charming had come back to me and I had no idea he was even alive.

XVI. RAPHAEL'S STORY

My life began in Kovno on June 21, 1918, as the second of three brothers.[1] As an engineer, my father was involved with importing advanced engineering systems from Germany into Lithuania. He introduced central heating systems into Lithuania as well as the packaging of meats into sausages. He was very successful until the rise of Hitler in Germany ended his good fortune. German companies no longer wanted to do business with him and the feeling was mutual. He then switched to importing building materials for construction companies. Unfortunately, due to his heavy smoking habit he passed away, in 1938, from lung cancer.

My mother was Russian and a pharmacist, who graduated from the University of St. Petersburg but gave up her profession to raise her children. My older brother, Misha, who eventually moved to Israel, attended university and was a construction engineer. He had a hobby as a glider and even though he was Jewish, he was accepted as a member of the Lithuanian Gliding Club. He was brilliant and published a magazine about gliding, learned English, and then published the magazine in English.

My younger brother, David, was born in 1921. David emigrated to the United States after my father died. I had just completed officers' school in the Lithuanian army and was mandated to stay in Lithuania for three years after the completion of school. This rule prevented my mother and me from joining David on his voyage to the United States.

All boys at the age of 17 had to serve in the army. Jews in the army were treated differently and weren't welcome in the army's society. Jews were looked upon as foreigners who had no place there. Nevertheless, there were a few Jewish higher-ups in the army: a Jewish colonial and a Jewish general, but the Jewish officers were mostly connected with the army's medical services.

We lived in Kovno, across the river was Slobodka, a district of mainly poor Jewish people. My family was not orthodox, but belonged to a temple and would attend services on religious holidays. My father, a cheder graduate, was more religious than my mother. My Russian mother didn't speak Hebrew. She spoke Russian and it was Russian that we spoke at home.

The Jewish population in Kovno didn't mix with the Lithuanians. I was the exception to the rule and went to a Lithuanian high school, while the majority of Jews went to Jewish or Hebrew schools. At my school all the subjects were taught in Lithuanian and as a token of good faith, once a month, they had a Jewish religion class.

After high school, I went to a military school with only four or five other Jews. I then went to the Lithuanian University where I was exposed to a sizable number of Lithuanians. The Lithuanians hated Jews but were able to hide their feelings well. This hatred manifested itself when, in the early 1930s, laws were passed to take wealth away from Jews and make it difficult for Jews to do business.

Lithuanians were mostly farmers and weren't very intelligent. When Lithuania won its independence in 1918 and because Lithuanian intelligence was low, they asked the Jews for help. A Jewish lawyer by the name of Robinson wrote the first constitution. There were many prominent Jews in the Lithuanian government at the time, but once the Lithuanians got used to their independence, they started to retrench the Jews from government and high official positions.

Trade was mostly controlled by Jews so the Lithuanians began directives to eliminate Jews from trade and to create Lithuanian companies that had certain privileges not given to Jews. In spite of all this, a certain percentage of the Jewish population remained quite comfortable, had businesses, and were professionals. There were, however, many Jews who weren't as fortunate.

We were aware of what was going on in Germany, but because it was in Germany, and not Lithuania, we were unconcerned with our safety, we were also unable to help in any way.

People were comfortable, had houses and businesses, and didn't want to lose everything they had worked so many years to obtain. During this time about two percent of the Jews left Lithuania, we, however, couldn't leave because of my army service. When Germany invaded Poland and started killing Jews, many Polish Jews came to Lithuania to go to the Japanese consulate in Kovno in order to apply for asylum.

Photographer unknown. *Portrait of Chiune Sugihara.*
1938. US Holocaust Memorial Museum.

In 1940, thousands of mainly Polish Jews lined up outside the consulate building to get foreign transit visas to leave Kovno. The Lithuanian Jews didn't pay much attention, thinking that Lithuania wouldn't be invaded. But the Polish Jews had witnessed Nazi atrocities in Poland and pleaded with Chiune Sugihara, a Japanese diplomat, to help them emigrate. Lithuanian Jews were ignorant of a German occupation experience.

At university, students were involved with fraternities and I joined a right-wing student fraternity, El-Al. There was a right-wing fraternity, a left-wing one, and one in between.

Many Jews at that time were communists and we were concerned with the fate of Jews in general. It was more difficult for Jews than Lithuanians to get medical licenses. Bribing, or knowing the right people, was an important way of life. Many young Jews didn't want to go into the army and, if they could afford it, would bribe someone to give them a deferment. There was an army colonial who, for a bribe, would fabricate medical conditions to excuse boys from army service.

Many people my age would go to universities in Europe and experience life elsewhere. Everybody had a dream of leaving Lithuania and going somewhere else. The United States was one of the more favorable places to go to.

In terms of cultural events, Kovno had a fairly prominent opera house with well-known singers. Opera was the center of all social activities. There was a Jewish theater, movies, a large university, and a school of medicine but the Lithuanians had their own societies and social organizations, separate from the Jews.

Our summers were spent in a bungalow in the country. My uncle, whose wife was my mother's sister, had a huge farm not too far from Kovno, and we spent a good deal of time there.

My family was comfortable until around 1934 or 1935. My father's health began to deteriorate, and by the time Russians came into power, we weren't doing well. The Russians created opportunities for Jews and many became professionals or went into family businesses.

When the Russians arrived, many felt that the antisemitism would lessen and allow Jews to become more carefree. The Russians did away with fraternities, which I missed very much. They introduced Russian history and language in all schools and universities. They deported successful business people, many of whom were Jewish, to Siberia. Everyone got more involved with their university studies because if you had a good education more opportunities were available to you.

I remember the day the Germans arrived because it was my birthday: June 21. I was at a party with friends and while coming home at 3 a.m., we noticed objects were falling from the sky. We thought people were perhaps throwing things out of planes but the next morning the streets were full of Red Army soldiers trying to escape the Germans.

Since the Lithuanian right-wingers cut off all forms of communication, we didn't know what was happening. Then the Lithuanian right-wingers released the prisoners, who had been incarcerated by the Russians, from jail.

These prisoners behaved like animals when they got out. They found weapons, put on white bands, and formed the Liberation Army of Lithuania. Their first job was to kill Jews and they not only went from house to house in Slobodka killing Jews but they went all over Kovno killing Jews. The next day, the German army moved in and issued an order for the Lithuanians to lay down their arms and take orders from the Germans.

My brother, who didn't look Jewish, was turned in by his best friend but he managed to escape, put on a white band, and went into hiding for two weeks. It was too late to make plans to leave Lithuania, but some managed to get to Sweden and Siberia.

Thousands of Jews were killed before the Germans even arrived in Kovno. They were taken to Fort VII and murdered. I only learned about what happened there when I arrived in the United States. All we knew was that they were taken somewhere and murdered. The Germans loved the Lithuanians because they were Jew-killing machines.

Every day there was a new announcement relating to Jews posted throughout the city. Signs indicating that all Jews should have yellow patches, that Jews weren't allowed to walk on sidewalks, that any business belonging to Jews should put a big sign saying as much and that Jews couldn't attend university. There were all kinds of rules and regulations and every morning we would run out to see new announcements hanging on buildings. Everybody was living in uncertainty of what would be announced next. The move into the ghetto was what was next.

The announcement that all Jews had to move into a ghetto in Slobodka eventually came and the Germans had us organize a Jewish Council, called the Ältestenrat, and elect a chief Jew called the Oberjude. Dr. Elkes was named the Oberjude.

The Ältestenrat had a reorganization committee that appointed relocation consultants. I was appointed as a relocation consultant, probably because I was a lieutenant in the Lithuanian army. I would be told who should be relocated into which houses and ready them for the move. It took three to four weeks to accomplish the move. There was no means of transportation, so the majority of people left the bulk of their furniture and possessions in their homes. Those who could afford it, bribed Lithuanians to help move their furniture.

The ghetto consisted of two sections, the big and the small ghetto. Everybody was assigned an apartment, formerly occupied by Lithuanians. They were mostly cheap, inexpensive private homes of three or four rooms and subsidized housing apartments.

We lived in a house with two rooms, probably because we knew somebody with a high rank. There was an outhouse but no running water. We had beds, pots, pans, clothes and books. My older brother was married and he and his wife lived with us.

The area looked like a small town in a western movie, with run down wooden houses and unpaved streets. There were a few stores but no lights on the streets and a seven or eight-story apartment building, without an elevator. There was a barbed wire fence that ran along the perimeter of the ghetto and one entry gate. The gate to the ghetto was opened to let workers in and out of, everybody was searched when they came back through the gate. The Lithuanian guards would kill anybody they saw trying to climb over the fence.

In the beginning, I was assigned to public works to make sure the roads were passable as well as ensuring other facilities were in good working condition. It was probably because I had a construction background. They assigned 20, mostly elderly people, to me. They wanted the roads to be fixed so they could transport Jews. Later, I was assigned to a team transporting lumber to ships, we would unload batches of lumber to take to a mill. I was the leader of my team. There were 30 men and 30 women in each team.

Before we were married, my wife Henny was in my team. Because we would go out in the country and cut wood, we made a deal with the farmers; we would give them money, clothes, or gold and they would give us food, such as potatoes or flour. I needed two or three people to distribute the food equally, so I assigned Henny to lead the group of distributors. I would check on her and that is how we got to know one another.

It was hard work, but not as hard as other jobs. The worst place to work was the airport. Workers would have to dig and carry heavy stones under harsh conditions. The guards were cruel and caused the deaths of many people. Our guards were more humane and they would often allow us to spend the night in a field when we traveled to the country. We would then load up the barges and go back to the city. This meant that we didn't have to constantly work.

Dr. Elkes put a person in charge of work details who would, when the Germans needed a particular number of people to do a type of job, be the one to select them. He was not a very honest person and ghetto people would bribe him to get better assignments. Dr.

Elkes, however, was honest and a good leader. He believed that negotiating with the Germans would get the best possible conditions for the Jews.

There was a Jewish police force that consisted of three precincts, each with its own captain and a chief of police, I believe. They superficially executed orders from the Germans and simultaneously carried out a certain amount of Underground work. They helped the Jewish population as much as they could but the Germans suspected them and killed the leadership at Fort IX.

Dr. Elkes' administration helped run the ghetto. Their obligation was to comply with orders given by the Germans and to execute these orders. They would negotiate terms with the Germans to try make life easier for Jewish people.

There were no schools and a primitive hospital. Officially, schools were illegal, so students would go to someone's house to be taught, about ten at a time. Food was brought in by trucks and distributed equally. There was a Jewish bakery and a Jewish butchery. Life consisted primarily of going to work and coming back. The ghetto was on the shores of a river and there was a little beach that people would visit and swim at for two or three hours. There was only one public bath in the ghetto, and you had to wait in line for it, so people would go to the river every week and swim instead.

People became more conscious of their Jewishness. There was a small temple in a very large tent across from the consul, in the village square, where public services were held. The barber, where I was married, was located in the tent as well as the notary public, where all papers and records were kept.

My brother was a member of the Underground. His main objective was to procure weapons. The police controlled the gate and would allow Underground members to enter and leave with weapons. They built up quite a reserve of weapons. When I went back to Kovno, years ago, my brother showed me where the warehouse was built; underground in a deep tunnel. They used to train Jewish partisans on how to use weapons and children were being trained, in shooting, to prepare them for when they went to Palestine. As shown in the picture below, underground members would hide weapons in all sorts of places, including deep wells that connected to the tunnels.

George Kadish. *Member of Kovno Ghetto Underground Hides Supplies in a Well*. 1942. US Holocaust Memorial Museum, courtesy of George Kadish/Zvi Kadushin.

When the Germans came to purge the small ghetto, people thought resistance was impractical and for the sake of self-preservation, many escaped to the big ghetto. The Germans, along with Lithuanians, came in with trucks, emptying each apartment and taking the inhabitants to Fort IX. About 3,000 people were killed and this was the first time the ninth fort was used to kill people.

Our relocation to the big ghetto, instead of to Fort IX, was down to luck. While I and my mother, brother, sister-in-law, and her brother waited in the line that would ultimately take us to Fort IX, my brother started to scream and push people in front of him. Some Lithuanians came over to shout at him but the Lithuanian in charge yelled at the other Lithuanians and told them to leave. As they walked away, we ran to the line that led to the big ghetto.

Sometime later, the Germans issued an order, we had to turn in all our gold and valuables. Many Jews used their gold coins to barter for food. The Germans went from house to house searching for gold, telling people to strip. They even had dogs that licked women's privates in search of gold. If the Germans found anything hidden on someone, they were shot.

My mother was sick and bedridden when we lived in the ghetto. She could barely walk but could still cook. The Germans had no concern for the sick, they only cared about laborers. In 1944, there was an Aktion that eliminated the sick, elderly, and children. No one anticipated this Aktion and while the young and healthy were at work, they came with buses, went from house to house, and took all the sick, elderly, and children. When I came home from work that day, I found out that my mother had been taken. Henny and my brother were home and had to carry her out to the bus that took her to Fort IX. After that Aktion, people hid the elderly and children.

I knew two people who were imprisoned at Fort IX and escaped. They were burying bodies and knew that they would be killed when they finished so escape was their only option. In 1944, word got around that the big ghetto was to be purged. People were building shelters in which to hide until the day of their liberation. One of these shelters, a long tunnel containing food and other necessities, was under an apartment building. We couldn't get into any of these shelters, so Henny and I made our own. Because it was a hole in the ground, we were discovered and sent to the trains.

We traveled for several days, in unsanitary conditions with screaming people, it was awful. The women got off in Danzig and then went on to Stutthoff and we continued to Dachau. We remained in Dachau for a few days before being relocated to Landsberg, where I was placed under forced labor, constructing barracks to shelter incoming prisoners. It was a new camp and they brought in masonite to use for walls, with straw on which to sleep. We would dig long trenches, place the masonite against the trench walls, lay the straw on the ground, and put on a roof, made of steel.

The Germans formed teams to build an underground factory in the woods, where they built Messerschmitt planes. We had to mix cement and dig ditches. It was grueling work and because we lacked sustenance, many got sick and died.

During a lineup, an announcement was made that all those with architectural or furniture making skills were wanted to volunteer for special duty. Even though I was standing next to a famous architect, from Kovno, who warned me that volunteering meant instant death, I raised my arm and told them that I was a carpenter. I recruited all the people who knew anything about building and assembling and became the head of a team that built living quarters, with furniture, for the families of the guards. I helped my father, brother, and anybody else I could. The guards would bribe me with cigarettes and extra food if I built extra furniture or gave preferential treatment to certain officers' requests.

My brother worked in a warehouse distributing uniforms. His job was not difficult and we were treated fairly.

The Landsberg camp had a hospital with Dr. Elkes in charge of it. In order to take care of the sick, Dr. Elkes needed medical equipment. He requested what he needed from the German authorities and they said they would take care of it. However, after several weeks, no medical supplies had arrived. Dr. Elkes said if they didn't take care of it by a certain date, he would go on a hunger strike. He went on his strike and died ten days later. I knew Dr. Elkes from the ghetto. He was our doctor. He was educated in Germany and had dedicated his life to medicine. He went to *chedar* with my father and showed me kindness while in the ghetto

During the winter of 1945, the Germans learned that the Soviet troops were advancing in the direction of our concentration camp and began marching us westward.

I woke up one morning, during our march, to find that all the German soldiers had deserted us. Moments before the American tanks arrived, we went to a nearby farmhouse, where we were given milk and bread. I believe the German farmer only helped us because he knew that the Americans were coming. Many Jews, because they were so unused to the rich food, got sick with diarrhea, and died. The food also made me sick, but I managed to survive.

The American soldiers transported us to a German air force academy building that had just been built nearby. The Americans had converted it into a recovery hospital and assigned us to rooms with doctors and nurses. The Germans were brought in to clean up the mess.

We were there for two to three weeks when it was announced that a train would take us back to Lithuania. I didn't want to go back there, but my brother did. At the train station, while Misha boarded the train, he told me to go and get food that was being distributed for the trip and by the time I got back from getting the food, the train had left.

Because I didn't want to go to Lithuania, I took another train and traveled to Dresden. There, I was stopped by Russian soldiers who accused me of being part of a resistance group. They put me in a camp where we dismantled German factories that were being sent to Russia. I was there for about a month before escaping, with the aid of a Russian Jewish soldier, through a hole in the fence.

I decided to travel to the British sector of Graz but was detained by the British and was prevented from going to Palestine. I was then released and allowed to relocate to Linz to look for my brother, the one who had emigrated to America years before and was serving as an officer in the US army. I contacted the American embassy in Linz and was offered an apartment.

I traveled to Lodz as I had heard that there were Lithuanian women there and hoped I might find Henny. When I got off the train in Lodz, I asked someone if he knew if Jewish women were there and he said there was an organization that was housing Jewish women before transporting them to Israel. He told me where to find the building and when I arrived, a woman standing in front of the building recognized me, from Kovno, told me that Henny was on the second floor. I eagerly went to the second floor and finally, after all the months of misery and incarceration, we were reunited at long last.

---

1. Aronson, R., *Oral history interview with Raphael Aronson*, Interviewed by: Randy M. Goldman, United States Holocaust Memorial Museum Collection, 1994

XVII. THE VOYAGE TO THE UNITED STATES

"We are alive. We are human, with good and bad in us. That's all
we know for sure.
We can't create a new species or a new world.
That's been done.
Now we have to live within those boundaries.
What are our choices?
We can despair and curse, and change nothing.
We can choose evil like our enemies have done and create a world
based on hate.
Or we can try to make things better."
Carol Matas

Even though I had planned to go to Israel, I realized that it was no longer possible. Ralph had family in America and he wanted to go there so we decided that we were going to start living again and not live in the past that had been beyond our control. Our past, when the world went mad, wouldn't ruin our future.

Hitler was a madman and caused his nation to go mad. It's terrible that people in power can motivate young people to become so beastly and live without any remorse.

So began our long journey to America.

We traveled, by train, from one European city to another, with the help of the Underground, following the partisans like children. The Russians wanted to remain in power and didn't permit Eastern Europeans to travel to the West.

We knew that David, Ralph's brother, was stationed in Austria and we wanted to get there. We even changed our surname to Aronsonis and posed as Greeks to get to Austria. It's remarkable how, under these conditions, the Underground news and information was very precise. We were traveling with another couple who went to Germany, where a large center for many in our situation was located.

When we arrived in Austria we wound up in Linz, but my brother-in-law was not there. He was running around Europe looking for us. He contacted a friend and asked him to wait for us. My husband got a job the next day in a center, sorting documents. In this center, they collected information from Germany about everything they had done to people, every prisoner they had in Germany as well as in the countries Germany occupied.

Ralph cataloged all this information and anything that had any information pertaining to Lithuania, he would put it to one side. Before we left Austria, Ralph asked his superior's permission to take the boxes of information he had put aside with him. Consequently, we came to America in 1947 with an enormous amount of information. In 1994 or 1995, Ralph contacted the Holocaust Museum and they collected all the information and interviewed us. Years later, my cousin visited the museum and asked to see the Aronson tapes. They were escorted upstairs and put in front of a television and watched all the interviews.

Living and working in Austria was not difficult for us, we both spoke German. In school, I studied German, English, Russian, Latin and of course, we spoke Lithuanian. We lived in a hotel where higher-ranking military soldiers were housed and I felt intimidated by these soldiers. I got a job as a receptionist in the hotel and would check military personnel in. We stayed in that hotel for a year before my brother-in-law found us. Knowing we wanted to go to the United States, he helped us get the proper documents and finally, we got the papers but had to go to Bremerhaven to await the legal invitation. There was a big strike by longshoremen on the waterfront which prevented us from leaving for the United States.

We went to Munich and stayed with some friends. We had friends all over Europe. I still had not gotten my period, but I thought it that was normal because of what I had gone through. Our friends insisted that I go see a doctor and see if anything was wrong. The doctor said I would eventually get my period but he also said that I was not pregnant and would have trouble conceiving as something was damaged from the hard labor I endured. I went back to our room and tearfully told my husband what the doctor had said, to which he replied, "What's the matter with you – I didn't marry you for children. I married you because I love you."

It turns out that the doctor was wrong. I was pregnant.

XVIII. THE TOMORROW OF YESTERDAY

"Our battered suitcases were piled
on the sidewalk again;
we had longer ways to go.
But no matter, the road is life."
Jack Kerouac

Years later, when I was in America, I received a letter from my cousin, Abrusha, who was my Aunt Shifra's son. He and his family had gone to Russia when news of the impending German invasion of Kovno reached them. Abrusha told me that his father met and married a young woman and was someplace in Russia with his wife.

Abrusha told me what had happened to his mother, Shiffra. She was trying to board a train to somewhere, perhaps Moscow or Leningrad, but security officials wouldn't let her board and she just disappeared. Shiffra told Abrusha to find me and tell me that she was there when my mother was cremated in Stutthof.

Misha had moved to Vilna and was quite important. Somehow Abrusha had found Misha, learned I was alive and was given my address. He wrote me a letter but sent it to a third party. I received a telephone call from this person who told me that he had a letter from Abrusha. I started talking with him and in his letter, he told me not to send him anything and that he would give me an address to send letters to. He was afraid of someone.

My husband and I went to Lithuania to see Misha. After Ralph and Misha were separated at the train station during the war, Misha went back to Lithuania. He had made plans with his wife as to where to meet after the liberation, unlike us, who never thought to do so. Misha was a very well-known engineer in Vilna. He was a communist and had a good life there, lots of money and privileges. His children grew up very comfortably and when we visited, their table was laden with wonderful food.

In 1989 we went to Lithuania for the second time. Ralph was determined to get Misha out of the country. Ralph and Misha regularly corresponded and Ralph kept telling Misha to get out, he felt it was no longer safe for him to live there. Finally, Misha decided to leave Lithuania. They had relatives in Israel who were involved with the government and these relatives got the whole family, of about ten people, into Israel and into apartments owned by the family.

Misha had no respect for Abrusha, saying he was very peculiar and paranoid. I always received letters from Abrusha and eventually, the letters stopped being mailed to a third party. He told me he was planning to move to Israel with his wife, who was a famous violinist. But, when his wife died and left him without any children, he moved to Israel, alone.

For a while, Abrusha did very well in Israel. He was well educated; growing up in Russia, Jewish parents used to tell their kids that if they didn't study hard, they would sweep the streets for the rest of their lives. Abrusha and I decided we would like to meet one another, so I went to Israel. I thought he was a nice person but I kept receiving letters from him saying that he didn't have enough money. We opened a bank account in Israel for him and I sent him money – not too much though as we had to help my brother-in-law as well.

Many Russian Jews came to America with a chip on their shoulder and believed, never hesitating to admit that the Jews of this America owed them something.

When I was volunteering for Brandeis University National Women's Committee in the 70s, a whole bunch of Russian Jews emigrated to Boca Raton and I was charged with assisting one family to integrate by taking them shopping, to the post office, and teaching them how to send letters. The husband, a former publisher for a Russian newspaper in Leningrad, was an exceptionally nice man, but he expected me to become his and his wife's best friend. It became so overwhelming that I had to end the association.

When we arrived in the United States we were welcomed by warm and loving relatives, Uncle Isaac, an established dentist, and his wife, Aunt Sissel. They owned an apartment in the Bronx. My aunt and uncle were charming people. Aunt Sissel was obsessed with actors and actresses and spent all her time reading magazines and attempting to look like the people inside. She loved beautiful people and I think, if I wasn't pretty, she would have sent me away.

We were there for two days when my aunt, unbeknownst to my uncle, came to my husband with a box of shoelaces and told him about a very good job available selling these laces. She told him all he had to do was to knock on doors, and people would buy the laces. He politely took the box and we realized we couldn't stay. We had to leave and find another apartment and jobs.

Ralph's cousin, who was an engineer and lived in another state, took him to Pratt Institute and they accepted him into the school. He went to Hias, the organization that helped Jewish refugees get settled in the United States, to ask them to cover the tuition as well as assist with living expenses. Hias agreed and told us to pay them back when we could.

Our uncle's dental office on Bryant Avenue was about ten blocks away from his Bronx apartment on Andrews Avenue. Attached to the office was a two-room apartment where they had lived before his success and subsequent move to a nicer neighborhood.

The apartment was vacant and, fortunately for us, we were able to move in. I had just given birth to my son and because the apartment was next to the waiting room of the dental office, I had to keep the baby very quiet but the patients found out that there were relatives from Europe living in the apartment with a baby. Waiting patients were always knocking on the door to see the baby and eventually I put gauze on the carriage and left the door open for them to see the baby.

Ralph attended school, full-time, and was given two years of credit from the schooling he had in Lithuania. Fortunately, he buried his school records when the Germans invaded and went back to dig them up after the war. He was very smart and always made a good impression so he had no problem getting jobs. He once worked as an architect for Barbara Bel Geddes' father but he soon realized that he wanted to do more than just architecture. To further his education, he went to Columbia and completed his master's degree.

In 1948, he came across an ad from a manufacturing company involved with X-ray shielding machines, looking for somebody who could design an X-ray shielding room, rather than the vests you wear in the dentist's office. The man, from Brooklyn, had his business in Manhattan and was so pleased when he hired Ralph. Ralph knew how to talk to doctors and people involved in hospitals and he did so well in his first year on the job that he received a very large bonus.

My husband developed his ideas, on how to shield larger places, all in a little office in Manhattan. When he turned 60, he decided to become an independent consultant. The United States government approached him and he began working at the Pentagon on some very large projects. He was the control manager of a 1.8 million dollar project comprising of the manufacturing of shielded components for anti-ballistic missile sites in Langdon, North Dakota. He was the author of several articles and manuals regarding shielding and environmental construction. He was a pioneer and renowned expert in his field of work.

The entire world wanted Ralph, we traveled extensively and Ralph had a top security clearance. When Bush was president, Ralph was sent to Iraq, he was a consultant for the Japanese government for ten years and was a consultant to the biggest construction company in Tokyo. I would always go with him when I could and there would always be a limousine waiting for us at the airport to take us to a fancy hotel. While staying at the hotel, a limousine would pick Ralph up every morning to take him to work. They would also send a car for me and take me anywhere I wanted to go.

I mentioned, once, that I would like to see flower arranging. Ralph's boss said that his wife, Osava, did flower arranging and invited us to lunch at his home. We were picked up and taken to his house and when we arrived, he asked us which dining room we would like to eat in: Japanese or Western. I said Japanese and he took us into a beautiful room that was designed like a stage where we sat on the floor on futons with a table in front of us. He put some soup on the table and I asked if he had any help, to which he responded that he liked to serve his best friends. The kitchen was in the basement and he used a dumbwaiter to get the food. Next, Osava did an exquisite flower arrangement with only a few flowers and their daughter came out and played the *koto*, a Japanese string instrument. It was quite an experience.

We also went to a Japanese wedding. The ceremony was held in a circle with the women on one side, wearing magnificent kimonos held together with netsukes. They stood with their fans open and when I said something in Japanese, instead of applauding, they waved their fans. I was told not to worry; the fans were waved instead of applauding.

We eventually settled in Stamford, Connecticut, and I gave birth to a daughter. My husband renewed his studies, graduated from Pratt Institute. After we were liberated and lived in Linz, I enrolled in an institute for physical fitness. I was always a natural athlete and I learned a good deal but I had to stop my studies due to my pregnancy.

In Stamford I took as many physical fitness classes as possible, but I didn't like the exercise machines they used. I mentioned this to Ralph and he helped me design my own class. I put a program together, with my own recorded music, and Ralph would critique where necessary. I started applying to teach my class in public schools but they wouldn't hire me because I didn't have a teacher's license.

A friend of mine told me that the Italian community center had built a magnificent studio in the gym, overlooking a beautiful pool. I applied there, they were impressed by my interview and hired me on a trial basis, just in case it didn't work out. I started on a Monday and was told that participants for the class would be provided.

When I walked in on that Monday morning, with my boom box, there were ten women waiting for me. They were all about ten years older than me and it turned out that they were the wives of the board of directors of the Italian community center. They all loved the class and I became so popular that I wound up instructing three times a week with 60 women in each class.

Unlike Mila, in Thane Rosenbaum's *Second Hand Smoke*, I was not going to pass the burden of my Holocaust experience on to my children, nor attempt to train them as Nazi hunters. We decided not to feed our children with our past, believing that a chance to live a better life in a new home should be our first priority. We learned to speak English and concentrated on being good Americans. If our children wanted to know more about what we went through, they could always ask us, or they could research on their own.

My son, Steven, an excellent student, was determined to know our life stories and in his search he acquired things that I didn't have or even knew existed. He found my number from Stutthof, not a tattoo but a number that the Germans assigned to you in their records. He gathered all the information from this period of our lives, much more than I have. I have so much hate for Lithuania but every time Steven went to Europe, he would visit Lithuania. He feels sorry for the handful of Jews left there, he sends them money and supports them but I feel his endeavors are wasted, the Jews that remain there don't even communicate, it's pathetic. They fight amongst themselves and have subsequently formed two factions.

The Japanese consul building, in Lithuania, was heavily damaged during the war and Steven funded its reconstruction into a museum. A plaque is on the building honoring his grandparents, Jacob and Tanya Aronson.

Mine has been a long, eventful, journey of heartbreak and discovery. Here I am today, almost 90 years old, having kept all these incredibly painful memories a secret, finally telling my tale. I have many mixed feelings about doing this, but at least our family, our grandchildren, will know something about that time. They have asked about it through the years, we tell them just enough but never offer more information. At least now they can go to the Holocaust Museum, press a button, and listen to their grandparents' account of the war – if they want to. It's okay If they don't want to, I only hope they grow up to be kind people. That's how we want them to be.

It's so painful to remember yesterday but I've finally reached tomorrow, the day after it all.

A MESSAGE OF LOVE
FROM HENNY'S DAUGHTER

Photographer unknown. *Ode to Life*. 1946. Henny: 2nd
from left, Courtesy of Steve Aronson.

*My mother had many secrets. This was not obvious to most people
as she was an extremely open and interesting conversationalist
but at home, she was the opposite.*

*Questions about her life, her past, her family, were always
answered but only partially. I was always left longing for more
information, more details. As a result, her life was a mystery to
me and I felt a need for more intimacy, to know her better, to get
closer.*

When I was a child, I read the diary of Anne Frank nearly every night. I really believed this was the story of my mother; that she, in some way, was my mother. This was how I got to know her better and I felt I got the glimpse that I needed into her life. It relaxed my need to know more and allowed me to appreciate her powerful and complicated life. Her mystery was intriguing, attractive, a little intimidating but most of all impressive.

She was elegant and everyone who knew her or met her could see that right away. She was very opinionated, especially about hair; my brother's hair, my hair, my friend's hair, the newscaster's hair, everybody's hair. She had terrific intuition and she was proud in the best use of the word. I do believe this was instrumental in her survival. She and her best friend in the concentration camp were singularly focused on cleanliness. They took care of each other, they washed each other and they inspected each other daily.

She expected a lot of the people she loved – but she demanded no less of herself. She was hard on us as children, but she was also hard on herself. She pushed herself to learn and keep learning. She stayed relevant and interesting. She didn't waste any time, not one minute. She was devoted to our father and she was a fierce defender of all of us.

After my father passed away, she struggled to make friends. He was truly her best friend and everyone else paled in comparison. She used to call her new friends her so-called friends. No one could really reach the bar she had set and she had a hard time trusting people. She didn't have much in the way of role models, no parents, and no siblings but she did the best she could, kind of winging it.

I know now, and appreciate, how powerful an extended family can be and how much it adds to the layers of one's life. To think that she missed all that is profoundly sad to me. I wish her life was different. I wish she had her mother, father, brother, cousins, uncles, aunts. I wish she had all those years as a beautiful young woman. I wish it wasn't taken from her.

Tina Aronson

SOURCE OF PHOTOGRAPHS

Photographs in public collections

The Body is Gone. United States Holocaust Memorial Museum. Available at: https://collections.ushmm.org/search/catalog/pa11842. George Kadish/Zvi Kadushin. Circa 1943.

Baltic Countries, 1933, Kovno Indicated. United States Holocaust Memorial Museum: Holocaust Encyclopedia. Available at: https://encyclopedia.ushmm.org/content/en/map/baltic-countries-1933. No Artist. No date.

Kovno environs, 1941-1944. United States Holocaust Memorial Museum. Available at: https://encyclopedia.ushmm.org/content/en/article/kovno. No Artist. No date.

Moving into the Kovno ghetto. United States Holocaust Memorial Museum Hidden History of the Kovno Ghetto. p. 53. George Kadish. 1941.

The Kovno Ghetto Jewish Council. Yad Vashem Photo Archives. Available at: https://photos.yadvashem.org/photo-details.html?language=en&item_id=100224&ind=2. Photographer unknown. 1943.

Jewish Forced Laborers Making Shoes. United States Holocaust Memorial Museum. Available at: https://encyclopedia.ushmm.org/content/en/photo/jewish-forced-laborers-making-shoes. Photographer unknown. 1943.

Portrait of Chaim Yellin. Yad Vashem Photo Archives. Available at: https://www.yadvashem.org/holocaust/this-month/january/1944.html. Courtesy of Avraham Tory. January 1944.

Group Portrait of Jewish Lithuanian Partisan Unit. US Holocaust Memorial Museum, courtesy of Eliezer Zilberis. Available at: https://encyclopedia.ushmm.org/content/en/photo/jewish-partisans-who-operated-in-forests-in-lithuania. Photographer unknown. 1944

Destruction of Kovno Ghetto. United States Holocaust Museum Hidden History of the Kovno Ghetto. p. 217. George Kadish/Zvi Kadushin. Circa August 1944 – October 1944.

Surviving Jews gathered outside the burnt remnants of the Kovno ghetto. Holocaust Education and Archive Research Team. Available at: http://www.holocaustresearchproject.org/revolt/gelpernusdiary8.html. Photographer unknown. 1944.

Portrait of Chiune Sugihara. United States Holocaust Memorial Museum. Available at: https://collections.ushmm.org/search/catalog/pa19502. Photographer unknown. 1938

Member of Kovno Ghetto Underground Hides Supplies in a Well. United States Holocaust Memorial Museum, courtesy of George Kadish/Zvi Kadushin. Available at: https://encyclopedia.ushmm. org/content/en/photo/member-of-the-kovno-ghetto-underground-hides-supplies-in-a-well. George Kadish. 1942

BIBLIOGRAPHY

Cassedy, Ellen, *We Are Here: Memories of the Lithuanian Holocaust*, University of Nebraska Press, 2012

Drywa, Danuta, *The Extermination of Jews in Stutthof Concentration Camp 1939-1945*, Panstwowe Museum Stutthof, 2004

Eilati, Shalom, *Crossing the River*, The University of Alabama Press, 2008

Elkes, *Joel Dr., Elkhanan Elkes of the Kovno Ghetto*, Paraclete Press, Mass., 1999

Faitelson, Alex, *The Truth and Nothing but the Truth*, Gefen Publishing House, 2006

Frome, Frieda, *Some Dare to Dream*, Ohio State University Press, 1988

Ganor, Solly, *Light One Candle*, Kodansha International, 2003

Gordon, Harry, *The Shadow of Death: The Holocaust in Lithuania,* The University Press of Kentucky, 1992

Greenbaum, Masha, *The Jews of Lithuania*, Gefen Books, 1995

Holocaust Education Research Team, *Einsatzgruppen A, Executions in Fort VII & Fort IX*, No Date

Klee, Ernst, Dressen, Willi & Riess, Volker eds, *The Good Old Days*, Konecky & Konecky, 1988

Levin, Dov and Brown, *Zvie The Story of an Underground*, Gefen Publishing House, 2014

Levine, Hillel, *In Search of Sugihara* The Free Press, 1996

Littman, Sol, *War Criminal on Trial*, Key Porter Books, 1993

Michaels, Anne, *Fugitive Pieces,* Alfred A. Knoff, New York, 1997

Mishell, William, *Kaddish for Kovno*, Chicago Review Press, 1988

Neitzel, Sonke and Welzer, Harald, *Soldaten*, Alfred A. Knopf, New York, 2012

Oral Testimony of Henny Aronson, United States Holocaust Memorial Museum

Oral Testimony of Raphael Aronson, United States Holocaust Memorial Museum

Oshry, Ephraim, *The Annihilation of Lithuanian Jewry*, The Judaica Press, 1995

Rapoport, Safira, *A Pedigreed Jew* The International Institute for Holocaust Research, Yad Vashem, Jerusalem, 2010

Rosner, Leo, *The Holocaust Remembered*, 1998

Schalkowsky, Samuel, ed. *The Clandestine History of the Kovno Jewish Ghetto Police,* Indiana University Press, 2014

Tory, Avraham, *Surviving the Holocaust: the Kovno Ghetto Diary*, Harvard University Press, 1990

United States Holocaust Memorial Museum, *Hidden History of the Kovno Ghetto*, Bulfinch Press, 1997

Zilber, Ettie, *A Holocaust Memoir of Love & Resilience. Mama's Survival from Lithuania to America*, Amsterdam Publishers, 2019

ABOUT THE AUTHOR

Dr. Dorothy Pierce is a retired educator and school administrator. After retirement, she became involved with Jewish organizations, most notably Brandeis University National Women's Committee and was national president for two years.

She instituted the Jewish Cultural Society at Florida Atlantic University in 2008 and served as its president from 2008 to 2012. Dr. Pierce served as president of the Gilda Malin chapter of Hadassah from 2011 to 2016 and now serves as vice president of the Gaela Atid chapter of Hadassah.

For the past four years, she has chaired the Jewish Cultural Club, a club that provides Jewish cultural programs to the members of her community: Boca Woods Country Club in Boca Raton, Florida. Besides her Jewish activities, Dr. Pierce serves on the board of Boca Woods PAP Corps., a South Florida organization that raises money for cancer research at the Sylvester Comprehensive Cancer Institute at the University of Miami.

She lives in Boca Raton, Florida with her husband Stanley, a retired college professor and attorney, who is also involved with several Jewish and civic organizations. Their two children, Leslie and Amy both live in California.

* * *

Dear Reader

Having written this biography of my friend Henny means a lot to me, and I feel grateful for the many positive comments it has received so far.

If you've enjoyed this book I would be very grateful if you could spend a few minutes leaving a review (it can be as short as you like) on the Amazon page.

Thanks a lot in advance!

HOLOCAUST SURVIVOR TRUE STORIES

The Series **Holocaust Survivor True Stories WWII**, by Amsterdam Publishers, consists of the following biographies:

1. Among the Reeds. The true story of how a family survived the Holocaust, by Tammy Bottner

Amazon Link: getbook.at/ATRBottner

2. A Holocaust Memoir of Love & Resilience. Mama's Survival from Lithuania to America, by Ettie Zilber

Amazon Link: getbook.at/Zilber

3. Living among the Dead. My Grandmother's Holocaust Survival Story of Love and Strength, by Adena Bernstein Astrowsky

Amazon Link: mybook.to/ManiaL

4. Heart Songs - A Holocaust Memoir, by Barbara Gilford

Amazon Link: <u>getbook.at/HeartSongs</u>

5. Shoes of the Shoah. The Tomorrow of Yesterday, by Dorothy Pierce

HOLOCAUST SURVIVOR MEMOIRS

The Series **Holocaust Survivor Memoirs World War II** , by Amsterdam Publishers, consists of the following autobiographies of survivors:

1. Outcry - Holocaust Memoirs, by Manny Steinberg

Amazon Link: getbook.at/Outcry

2. Hank Brodt Holocaust Memoirs. A Candle and a Promise, by Deborah Donnelly

Amazon Link: getbook.at/Brodt

3. The Dead Years. Holocaust Memoirs, by Joseph Schupack

Amazon Link: getbook.at/Schupack

4. Rescued from the Ashes. The Diary of Leokadia Schmidt, Survivor of the Warsaw Ghetto, by Leokadia Schmidt

Amazon Link: getbook.at/Leokadia

5. My Lvov. Holocaust Memoir of a twelve-year-old Girl, by Janina Hescheles

Amazon Link: getbook.at/Lvov

6. Remembering Ravensbrück. From Holocaust to Healing, by Natalie Hess

Amazon Link: getbook.at/Ravensbruck

7. Wolf. A Story of Hate, by Zeev Scheinwald with Ella Scheinwald

Amazon Link: getbook.at/wolf

8. Save my Children. An Astonishing Tale of Survival and its Unlikely Hero, by Leon Kleiner with Edwin Stepp

Amazon Link: getbook.at/LeonKleiner

9. Holocaust Memoirs of a Bergen-Belsen Survivor & Classmate of Anne Frank, by Nanette Blitz Konig

Amazon Link: getbook.at/BlitzKonig

10. Defiant German - Defiant Jew. A Holocaust Memoir from inside the Third Reich, by Walter Leopold with Les Leopold

Lightning Source UK Ltd.
Milton Keynes UK
UKHW041928040721
386628UK00001B/58